...ERICA, DIVIDED INTO COUNTYES, TOWNSHIPS AND LOTTS

Surveyed by Tho. Holme Sold by P. Lea at ye Atlas and Hercules in Cheapside

...es in Length and one in Breadth

Delaware River

To William Penn Esqr
Proprietor & Governer of
PENN-SYLVANIA
This Mapp is humbly Dedicated
and Presented.
by Ino Harris

References to the Settlements of
Severall Inhabitants in ye Countyes of
BUCKS and PHILADELPHIA

1	Ino Parsons	1	Ind Stille
2	Lin Brinlow	2	Lake Brinslo
3	Wm Buck	3	Hen Lones
4	Wm Biles	4	And Boelson
5	Iosi Bore	5	Ausi Inshewson
6	Ro Lucas	6	And Peterson
7	Gd Wheeler	7	Sweeds Mill
8	Int Haycock	8	Omcrest Cock
9	Into Wheeler	9	And Boon
10	Tho Marle	10	Pet Eliot
11	Wm Paxton	11	Walt Dalbo
12	Iam Paxton	12	Ind Hunt
13	Ino Flackne	13	Enochson
14	Wid Marsh	14	Edw Opdram
15	Rich Thatcher	a	Tho Cross
16	Ino Karbrow	b	Giles Knight
17	Nic Walho	c	Ann Salter
18	Ino Tawn	d	Erick Meels
19	Clem Dungan	e	Peter Kambo
20	Mor Bowden	f	Neels Nelson
21	Wm Dungan	g	Rich Wall
22	Rio Lundy	h	Rush Wall
23	Tha Dungan	i	Eo Dalton
24	Ino Tully	k	Wm Brown
25	Wm Mouge	l	Ind West
26	Wid Walmsley	m	Ind Bunts
27	Ann Clarke	n	Phi Lahuman
28	Rich Noble	o	Ind Lownet
29	Iac Pedison	p	Erickscock
		q	Wm Salwuy
		r	Geo Foreman
		s	Mouns Cock
		t	Grif Iones
		u	Ind Cook
		x	Wm Salwuy
		y	D Factory

The Dutch Township

COUNTY OF PHILADELPHIA

PLYMOUTH Township

GERMAN Township

Penn Jun Man of Williamstadt

Gulielma Maria Penns Man of Springfeld

SOCIETY

Mannor of Springets berry

Philadelphia

THE SOCIETY LAND

THE COUNTY OF BUCKS

MANNOR OF MORELAND

The Proprietrs MANNOR OF HIGHLANDS

New Town

The Proprietryes Mannor of ye Pennsbery

Bridlington

NEW JARSEY

STONE HOUSES

Traditional Homes of Pennsylvania's Bucks County and Brandywine Valley

STONE HOUSES

Traditional Homes of Pennsylvania's Bucks County and Brandywine Valley

PHOTOGRAPHY BY GEOFFREY GROSS

TEXT BY
MARGARET BYE RICHIE
JOHN D. MILNER
GREGORY D. HUBER

RIZZOLI
NEW YORK

To my good friend Mead Shaffer and his res-
olute effort to preserve historic Pennsylvania;
to my parents Joan & Mark; and, as before,
for Alice—still my little girl.
              — Geoffrey Gross

First published in the United States of America in 2005 by
Rizzoli International Publications, Inc.
300 Park Avenue South, New York, NY 10010
www.rizzoliusa.com

ISBN: 0-8478-2687-2
LCCN: 2005900673
© 2005 Rizzoli International Publications, Inc.

Photographs, as well as essay on 166 © 2005 Geoffrey Gross

Foreword, as well as essays beginning on pages 26, 46, 58, 64, 68, 74, 78, 84, 94, 132, 140 © 2005 Margaret Bye Richie

Introduction, as well as essays beginning on pages 38, 106, 116, 124, 200, 212 © 2005 John D. Milner

Essays beginning on 32, 88, 100, 148, 152, 158, 162, 166, 168, 174, 180, 184, 189, 194, 206, 218 © 2005 Gregory D. Huber

Essay beginning on page 52 © 2005 Stephen Phillips

Essay beginning on page 144 © 2005 Herbert H. Michel, DD/Pastor

Note: Captions accompanying each essay were written by the author of that essay (author indicated by initials following each essay), with the exception of the captions for Old Trappe Church, which were written by Gregory D. Huber, and those for The Armitage House, which were written by John D. Milner.

Designed by Abigail Sturges

Printed and bound in U.S.A.

2005 2006 2007 2008 2009 / 10 9 8 7 6 5 4 3 2 1

Front cover: The Schilling Residence, "Florin" (p. 124)

Back cover: A house in the Delaware River Valley plays host to a handsome Hadley chest made about 1700 in the Connecticut River Valley. The framed needle and bead-work piece, silver tankards, monteith, porringers, and salt glaze *sack* bottles were made in London in the seven-teenth century, and could have been found in fine colonial homes in Philadelphia and Boston.

Page one: Newlin Grist Mill (p. 174)

Pages 2–3: Garrett-Booth-Cheyney House (p. 168)

Contents

Above: Diamond corner notching of stripped logs used here in the Southey House was unusual in southeastern Pennsylvania.

Facing page: Nails seen on vertical exterior boards of open door attach to horizontal interior facing battens. Chest and trestle table are of earliest design. The windsor chair is of 1780 to 1800.

Foreword

Margaret Bye Richie

Buildings, like poems and rituals, realize culture.
    —*Henry Glassie in* Vernacular Architecture

The founding of Pennsylvania was an extraordinary event, pertinent to but not altogether presaging the proliferation of stone houses that took shape during the first hundred years in this new colony. These dwellings have been fortuitous byproducts of the overall success of what was known as Penn's Holy Experiment. Our book supports this development through cataloguing the built environment that qualified the lives of the colonists who followed Penn. It seeks also to describe the buildings as manifestations of the cultures from which these colonists emerged.

Arrival in the New World was evidence that our forefathers, who were both courageous and ambitious, had acted out of a desperate desire to escape from many limiting factors in their native lands. They had a fairytale-like confidence that a new start in Pennsylvania would free them from restrictions that for centuries had plagued all but the very privileged in the countries from which they were fleeing. They believed that with hard work and good luck, freedom of worship and upward mobility would be the concomitant reward.

William Penn, the founding father, of English-Dutch stock, was the son of Admiral Sir William Penn (1621–1670) to whom Stuart King Charles II owed a large debt for supplies and services. Upon the death of his father, William the younger persuaded the King to pay off this debt with lands in the New World. Charles agreed and Penn became single owner of a vast spread of territory between the lands held under the Duke of York (what is

Interior of a log house cooking area exhibits late-seventeenth- and eighteenth-century furniture. Above the fireplace, the simple mantel is typical of those seen in certain late-eighteenth- and early-nineteenth-century houses in southeastern Pennsylvania.

now New York and New Jersey) and Maryland. How far this forested land stretched westward was not determined.

Although young Penn was the scion of an admiral, when as a youth he heard George Fox, a contentious Quaker, preach love, peace, and tolerance, he ended his membership in the Church of England to follow the Quaker leader. There were thousands of others in Great Britain and on the continent who were also at odds with their established churches and longed for a change. They were to become the players in a plan that was forming in the mind of Penn.

He set about defining a frame of government for the new colony he would establish on the west bank of the Delaware River for those who wished to escape the indignities foisted upon them in their mother lands. Publishing and distributing hundreds of pamphlets and broadsides throughout Great Britain and Western Europe, he advertised the low price of land and the freedoms and opportunities to be had in "Pennsylvania" (the name that the King had declared the only suitable one for the lands he had granted this eager young reformer). When, in the ship

Welcome, accompanied by early settlers, in 1682 he landed in Philadelphia, he found only a few Swedes, Finns, and Dutch inhabiting log cabins and on friendly terms with the Lenni Lenape Indians who had roamed the forests for centuries. The overall inspiration and hope of these aspiring immigrants who had the courage to cross the Atlantic lay in the knowledge that before departure each had been issued a warrant on a piece of land, paid for but as yet not surveyed. Acting on the terms of his declared principles for acquisition of land, Penn further insisted that newcomers negotiate fairly with the Native Americans any object or lands they wished to buy. This provision for fairness underlay to a comforting degree the good relations that Pennsylvanians had with the Native Americans for the first fifty years (until 1737).

Other ambitious Europeans had preceded Penn in venturing to the New World. None had possessed the drive and good fortune of Pennsylvania, which sprang from the spirit of William Penn and his settlers. Historically, Penn was by far the most successful promoter of a colony, even though

Steps lead upward into a spiral staircase, sometimes called a winder, leading to the "garret." The open door at right reveals a room that uses the outside log work without surfacing the interior of the wall.

Corner diamond notching like this example builds a sturdy house.

his physical presence in the Delaware Valley was brief. Immigrants by hundreds, then thousands, poured into Pennsylvania. Denominations of almost all faiths: Quakers and Baptists from Wales and England; Presbyterian Scots from Ulster; Mennonites from the Rhineland; and many others spread out in the townships around. His Holy Experiment was based on a government that had no army or artillery, yet Pennsylvania was to materialize into the most flourishing and exciting colony the New World had yet experienced. The dream for a better life had set out to speak for itself.

FIRST SHELTERS

Shelter in the Delaware Valley was at first rudimentary. In the Philadelphia area, arriving settlers utilized the steep banks of the river or newly dug caves, closing openings to the weather with whatever they could find: logs, sticks, canvas, and the like. Sod walls and roofs could be transferred from the ground onto wood supports set in place.

With the help of the Lenapes and the established settlers most newcomers made immediate plans to locate the land described on their warrants. This entailed an arduous trip along established Indian paths through the forests with camping stops along the way.

All must have wished to build the log type of house they had seen as soon as they debarked. Fortuitously, the forests were generously supplied with timber, some already on the ground. Two strong men could make a small clearing in a suitably chosen rise of the land, then wield axes to cut logs, strip and notch these at the ends, erect walls leaving an opening for a chimney, saw out window openings, cover the roof area with temporary bark, withes or sod, then possibly build simple supports for bunks in twenty-four hours. Later, the walls could be made weather-tight and improvements attempted to assure a snug and satisfying home. Penn, himself, endorsed log houses, offering a floor plan and room sizes close to Swedish prototypes. Documentation about Delaware Valley log houses between 1625 and 1700 indicates a rude and comfortless mode of

life. Even so, such log houses predominated in Pennsylvania for over a hundred years. Documents verify a count of ninety-eight-percent log houses in one rural township, Plumstead, which recorded its house types in 1798.

This high percentage of log dwellings should not suggest that settlers did not think about building more substantial and permanent homes. Evidence that this hope would be realized is ubiquitous. Almost all farmers found themselves surrounded by fieldstones, or in some areas actually living on top of limestone, which enriched the soil. Many of these owners, anticipating a house of stone some years in the future, began piling them up. Eventually, it would be possible to erect a one or two-room long house with internal gable-end chimneys. In the absence of architects, individuals would rely on their experience and their memory of traditional homes in their respective motherlands.

Impetus added to desire grew naturally out of the fortunate position in which most farmers found themselves. With the presence of a rock supply, which might consist of sandstone, limestone, shale or the ever-hard quartzite, was the realization that when a farmer felt ready, he could build an adequate house.

Early in the eighteenth century, settlers began earnestly to build the houses now so admired in the mid-Atlantic region. Men used the supplies at hand. The wood for floors, window frames, flooring, and stairs was the most expensive component required. Fortune smiled on these immigrants in the Delaware Valley once again, offering forest growth that reached west as far as the prairies.

By 1750, the use of limestone was fully understood. With the rich, fertilizing qualities of lime and the promise of stone, a wealth of opportunities was available to the ambitious farmer. In consequence, industrious farmers also built outbuildings such as smoke houses, spring houses, wash houses, out-kitchens and barns as well as sturdy houses.

Together with the reality of a home and outbuildings, it was the ambition of most settlers to own their land. The inspiration and hope of these travelers rested in the knowledge that before departure they had been accorded a grant of land drawn on a map by Penn's surveyor. Time, patience, and determination were the touchstones needed, and which these settlers possessed. By the end of the colonial period many had achieved ownership. The year 1776 established the fact that approximately ninety percent of the 2.5 million Americans lived on their own farms.

10

Introduction

John D. Milner

My interest in early domestic architecture of the Delaware Valley was piqued in the 1960s when I was working as an intern for the Historic American Buildings Survey in Philadelphia and had the opportunity to see the results of the Chester County project that had recently been completed. The purpose of that project was to document, with photographs and written histories, a representative sampling of the most significant private and public architecture in the county from the early eighteenth century through the late nineteenth century. The superb photographs were taken by Ned Goode and the research was undertaken by the Chester County Historical Society under the direction of Bart Anderson.

I was also intrigued by two marvelous books, *Early Domestic Architecture of Pennsylvania* by Eleanor Raymond (published in a limited edition of 1100 by William Helburn, Inc., New York, 1931) and *Bucks County, Photographs of Early Architecture* by Aaron Siskind, with text by William Morgan (published by Horizon Press for the Bucks County Historical Society, 1974). I purchased a first edition of the Raymond book at an auction in Philadelphia in 1962. The Siskind/Morgan book was a gift from my parents. What struck me about the photographs in both of these books was their documentary quality. There did not appear to be a conscious attempt by the photographers to style the images to create idealized situations. The subjects, whether exterior views of houses, barns or meeting houses, or interior views of fireplace walls, stairways or woodwork, were permitted to speak for themselves and provide an important and unedited historical record of vernacular architectural precedent in the Delaware Valley.

I first became aware of the work of architectural photographer Geoffrey Gross through the book *Dutch Colonial Homes in America* (published by Rizzoli International Publications, Inc., New York, 2002). Geoffrey Gross's splendid photographs captured the essence of the distinctive architecture created by early settlers from the Netherlands.

This sheep barn in Chester County, designed by John Milner Architects, was constructed in 1994. The roof was thatched by William Cahill using water reeds harvested from wetlands in Cape May County, New Jersey, and wheat straw from Lancaster County, Pennsylvania.

In *Stone Houses: Traditional Homes of Pennsylvania's Bucks County and Brandywine Valley*, Geoffrey Gross's images carry on the documentary tradition of Eleanor Raymond and Aaron Siskind, at a very high artistic level. His photographs have a wonderfully simple and serene quality, capturing the intrinsic nature of the buildings and their details in beautifully crafted compositions. One can feel the history, spirit, and atmosphere of each building, and appreciate the skill and artistry of those who created it.

I was delighted by the invitation to write an introduction to *Stone Houses*. My career has been devoted to the study and preservation of the region's architectural heritage, and I have had the opportunity to participate in the restoration of many of the buildings included in this volume. In fact, my wife and I live in one that we have restored, the 1724 Abiah Taylor House in East Bradford Township, Chester County. What first drew me to these buildings was the craftsmanship employed in their construction. I was fascinated by the raw materials and the techniques used to give those materials shape and purpose within a building. I felt a connection with the craftsmen and with their thought processes as design concept flowed into completed work. Geoffrey Gross's photographs bring those connections alive for me.

The four suburban counties that border Philadelphia—Bucks, Montgomery, Delaware, and Chester—possess an incredibly rich collection of vernacular architecture created in the formative years of the new nation by a diverse group of settlers from Sweden, England, Scotland, Ireland, Wales, Germany, Switzerland, The Netherlands, and France. As could be expected, these settlers in the late seventeenth and early eighteenth centuries designed and built their buildings based in large measure on what they had experienced in their countries of origin, using materials that were readily available. The result was a vernacular architectural palate that expressed the cultural diversity of those who had ventured to the New World. The term *vernacular* describes architecture that is "of the place" in terms of design and materials, and not superimposed, subscribing to styles and values that are foreign to the place. A modest fieldstone house by a stream is vernacular; a six-story Federal courthouse in the Beaux Arts style is not.

As David Hackett Fischer points out in his book, *Albion Seed*, by 1700 the English and Welsh colonists were by far the predominant group, comprising more than one-half of the total population. The vast majority of these English-speaking immigrants were Quakers or Quaker sympathizers. The impact of their belief system, their lifestyle, and their architecture would shape the character of the region for decades and centuries to come.

The history of the founding, growth, and maturity of this country is documented in many ways—through the written record, the graphic record (drawings, sketches and, after the 1850s, photographs), and the archeological record. It is also documented in fine arts, decorative arts, furniture, and technology. The most accessible form of documentation, however, is architecture—the buildings that exist in our environment. Every day we have access to the architectural record, without having to go to a library or a museum, by just walking down the street or driving along a country road. The architectural record is much more than simply a collection of styles that reference a particular time period or cultural influence. It is also a catalog of building materials, and the technology employed in their fabrication and assembly, that places each structure in the context of the nation's development from initial settlement through the Industrial Revolution and beyond.

Except in rare instances, the creation of architecture is not a private exercise of a particularly talented or inspired individual, as is the case, for instance, with poetry, painting and sculpture. Architecture requires the collective efforts of owners, designers, builders, and specialized craftsmen, and is dependent on the availability of materials and the technology to shape and assemble those materials to make a building.

The Caleb Pusey House on the west bank of the Chester Creek in the Borough of Upland, Delaware County, is perhaps one of the best examples of the fact that the earliest settlers built their buildings using the precedents established in their native lands. Caleb Pusey was a Quaker who lived in the village of Upper Lambourne, Berkshire. He departed England and arrived in the Delaware Bay aboard the *Welcome*, a small vessel in a large group of ships that made the journey to the new land between 1682 and 1685. Pusey set up a milling operation on Chester Creek in 1682 and built a modest house using local fieldstone and a limited amount of brick.

While working part-time in the early 1960s for John Miller Dickey, a highly respected architect and personal mentor practicing in Media, Pennsylvania, I had the good fortune to be assigned to the Pusey House restoration project. It was my first hands-on experience with investigating and documenting a historic building that, because of its early date, had little precedent in the region for its architectural form and details. I spent many weekends staring at the building and measuring its various parts in an effort to

Careful study of woodwork details is helpful in establishing the construction chronology of early buildings. This beautifully carved original door surround of the Burges-Lippincott House in Historic Fallsington, Bucks County, is consistent with the Federal style of the early nineteenth century.

determine what it had looked like in 1682, and how it had changed over time. I found that trying to place myself in the minds of the craftsmen who worked on the building led me to an understanding of the logic and sequence of construction. A trip to Upper Lambourne, with visits to the very early thatched roof stone cottages that must have been known to Caleb Pusey, provided just the precedent I was seeking, and proved to be invaluable for interpreting the architectural evidence I was finding in the Pusey House.

There is documentation for the use of thatched roofs in America in the very early colonial period. Thatched roofs were outlawed in Boston in the 1630s because of a concern for fire. The use of water reed, available in wetland areas along the East Coast, was the favored material because of its durability and relatively long life. Thatch gave way to wood, clay tile, slate shingles, and sheet metal as materials for covering roofs. In recent years, there has been a renewed interest in thatching for use on residences, garden houses, and farm buildings.

While this book focuses primarily on stone buildings, brick was a widely used material for construction in the Delaware Valley, particularly in areas where natural clay deposits could be found. In the early days of settlement, prior to the establishment of commercial brickyards, hand-molded bricks for the construction of houses were often made right on the site in small temporary kilns. Several significant houses constructed of brick are included in this book, among them the Samuel Levis House, Barns-Brinton House, Abiah Taylor House, Primitive Hall, Pennsbury Manor, and a section of the Thomas Massey House. Another brick building, remarkable in its three-story configuration, is the William Miller House in Avondale, Chester County.

The Thomas Massey House in the Township of Marple, Delaware County, is an excellent example of the evolution of a simple Pennsylvania farmhouse over a time span of three centuries. The earliest section of the house, a small log or wood frame structure, was standing in 1696 when Thomas Massey erected a handsome brick addition. In the second quarter of the eighteenth century, the original section was replaced by a more substantial stone addition that was later expanded in at least two increments during the eighteenth and nineteenth centuries. This linear pattern of expansion is typical of early houses in the Delaware Valley, and is a contributing factor to their "additive" character.

Documenting the physical evolution of early buildings is quite challenging, and often involves a variety of coordinated techniques including archival research, physical investigation of the architectural fabric, and archeological excavations. With the Massey House, all three techniques yielded critical information on which to base a thorough and accurate restoration. The leaded glass windows in the 1696 section are a case in point. An inventory compiled at the time of Thomas Massey's death in 1707 listed a quantity of "unwrought walnut" in an outbuilding. When I removed a clearly modern board from one of the large window surrounds in the brick section of the house, I discovered that portions of the original solid walnut casement window frame had survived largely intact. Nail holes in grooves on the outer portions of the frame indicated that the original window glass had been four inches wide and six inches high and had been fixed in place. Archeological excavations yielded many pieces of the original lead cames that secured rectangular panes, as well as fragments of original window glass that, when re-assembled, measured four inches by six inches. On a trip to Thomas Massey's likely home village of Nantwick, near Marpoole, in Cheshire,

Above: The first two stories and rear wing of the William Miller House were built in 1730, and the third story was added in 1771. Restored in 1964 with the guidance of architect Penelope Hartshorne Batchelor, the missing second floor plaster cove cornice, first floor pent roof and the front entrance stoop were reconstructed.

Facing page, top: The original kitchen in the 1730 rear wing of the William Miller House was reconstructed on the basis of careful research and the interpretation of surviving architectural evidence.

Facing page, bottom: The original fireplace mantel in the east parlor on the first floor of the William Miller House was restored to its 1730 appearance, and the missing original cabinet to the right was reconstructed.

Portions of the large original window frame in the 1696 Massey first floor room had survived, indicating that it had been divided into six parts, each with a panel of leaded glass. The lower part at the center contained a hinged window sash; the other panels had been fixed in place.

Recreation of the casement windows in the Abiah Taylor House was based, as with the Thomas Massey House, on archeology that produced surviving fragments of original window glass and lead cames.

England, I discovered early brick houses with casement windows, glazed with panes measuring four inches by six inches.

The information gained as a result of the casement window restoration at the Thomas Massey House proved to be of significant value in my work on the restoration of the 1714 Barns Brinton House in Pennsbury Township, Chester County, and my own house, built in 1724 for Abiah and Deborah Taylor in East Bradford Township, Chester County. Both of these buildings were built of hand-molded red brick and featured leaded glass casement windows of varying sizes.

Very few early buildings escape the inevitable alteration and expansion resulting from successions in ownership, evolving needs and tastes of the occupants, and even changes in function. The John Moland House, built circa 1755 in Warwick Township, Bucks County, gained historical significance when it served as General George Washington's headquarters in 1777 during a two-week encampment of the Continental Army. It was there that General Washington met with the Marquis de Lafayette and Count Pulaski before moving on to the Battles of Brandywine and Germantown, and the winter at Valley Forge.

Restoration of the Moland House, undertaken by the Warwick Township Historical Society with guidance by my business partner Mary Werner DeNadai, is planned for completion in early 2005. As part of an extensive archival, architectural, and archeological research project, the building's secrets were revealed, including evidence of a missing and massive original cooking fireplace with a stone sink. Geoffrey Gross's photographs are particularly valuable because they document the building during the restoration process.

The earliest stone houses of the Delaware Valley were built of local stone recovered from farm fields after being brought to the surface by plowing or by centuries of erosion and winter freeze. Referred to as "fieldstone," the individual pieces had weathered faces and were of random size and shape. When laid up in a wall by masons, the pattern of the stonework was often random, also called "rubble." Sometimes an owner or builder wished to have a more regular pattern of stonework in his facades, and had the stone laid in horizontal bands or courses, referred to as "ashlar". This ashlar pattern can be seen on the front facades of the Henry Melchior Muhlenberg and Peter Wentz Houses. When the technology of extracting stone from the ground by mechanical means was developed in the late eighteenth and early nineteenth centuries, quarries were established and the resulting stone pieces

Above: Built circa 1755, the John Moland House was expanded incrementally through the 1940s. The partially whitewashed first floor wall of the lower stone wing represents the 1760 one-story kitchen, raised in height in 1858.

Left: In this view, restoration of the exceptionally large cooking fireplace in the 1760 kitchen of the John Moland House is nearing completion. The built-in stone sink drains through a small hole in the exterior wall.

Serpentine fieldstone was laid in a random or "rubble" pattern to construct this handsome spring house on a farm near West Chester in the early nineteenth century. Recently restored, the building now serves as a private chapel.

could be shaped or "dressed" to facilitate more formal facades.

Because of the difficulty in transporting heavy stone, most early masonry buildings utilized material that was readily available in that locality. Granite, sandstone, and limestone were available in different regions of the Delaware Valley. A rather unique stone, known as Serpentine, could be found in the vicinity of West Chester, Chester County. It was accessible as fieldstone in the mid-eighteenth century, and became available from several quarries during the late eighteenth century and throughout the nineteenth century. Its distinctive green and blue-green color was regarded as appealing, and the material was used in a number of houses and commercial and institutional buildings.

As was the case with English settlers, immigrants from Germany who settled in the Delaware Valley in the early eighteenth century brought with them knowledge of the building traditions in their homeland. Their first buildings reflected the overall form and specific details with which they were familiar. However, by the middle of the century the English aesthetic began to influence and eventually dominate the trend in domestic vernacular architecture in the American colonies, leading to the creation of what is known as the "colonial" style.

The Henry Melchior Muhlenberg House, located in the village of Trappe, Montgomery County, was built between 1750 and 1755 by John Jacob Schrack, the son of immigrants from Germany. Although clearly influenced by the English architectural aesthetic prevalent in the region, the house has decidedly Germanic characteristics including the "half hall" floor plan arrangement, cast iron five-plate heating stoves, arched interior window reveals, and thermal insulation, known as "paling," installed between the first floor joists.

The Peter Wentz House, located in Worcester Township, Montgomery County, was completed by 1758 and gained historical significance because of its association with General Washington. Specific architectural characteristics, such as the attached summer kitchen and the incredibly exuberant interior painted decoration, reflect the German heritage of the Wentz family. However, the building's Georgian features, such as the center hall plan, symmetrical facade, prominent balcony, and pent roofs, attest to the blending of English and German styles.

The remarkable design and craftsmanship of the early English and German settlers has had a significant impact on design in this country for the past three centuries. The

This whimsical painted decoration in the Peter Wentz House was discovered on the original plaster wall surfaces, long concealed by later layers of paint and wallpaper.

The original fireplace woodwork in the parlor of 1714 Barns-Brinton House in Chester County features bold profiles for the bolection molding, frieze and mantel shelf.

This fireplace mantel at Peaceable Farm in Bucks County, designed by Richardson Brognard Okie, illustrates the architect's highly personalized interpretation of early colonial woodwork details.

proportions, materials, and details employed by these artisans appeared and reappeared as architects and builders searched for an architectural vocabulary that best fulfilled their image of America. Although that image was clouded during the nineteenth century by a desire to achieve sophistication through adoption of European fashions in design, the colonial architectural spirit boldly emerged again in the early twentieth century and has endured in one form or another ever since.

Architect Richardson Brognard Okie (1875–1945) was at the forefront in "re-discovery" of the colonial style in the Delaware Valley. Mr. Okie's interpretation of the Pennsylvania farmhouse, with its additive qualities, was unique. His work indicates a passion for proportion, architectural detail and fine craftsmanship. He drew heavily on the exterior massing and the configuration of wood paneling and moldings found in eighteenth- and early-nineteenth-century vernacular buildings, often interpreting their design at a diminutive scale.

I have had the pleasure of working on the restoration of many "Okie houses." In the process, I have examined copies of hundreds of his original architectural drawings that document, in painstaking detail, every conceivable aspect of a building. It is difficult to imagine finer examples of Mr. Okie's highly personal residential designs than the Schilling Residence in Montgomery County and Peaceable Farm in Bucks County, captured in Geoffrey Gross's exquisite photographs.

Architect G. Edwin Brumbaugh (1890–1983) enjoyed a long career in the Delaware Valley, specializing in the restoration of historic buildings and the design of new buildings influenced by eighteenth century vernacular precedent. Mr. Brumbaugh had a deep appreciation for the inherent architectural and structural rationale of early buildings and, in my opinion, his work reflects a desire to honor the eighteenth century craftsmen and "do it the way they would have done it." That phrase is one I have heard quoted many times by individuals who knew and worked closely with Mr. Brumbaugh.

The early vernacular architecture of southeastern Pennsylvania has had a profound influence on my own work for the past three decades. The treasures of this region afford almost limitless inspiration for the restoration of historic buildings as well as for the design of new buildings in the context of an exceptional landscape. The more I work on these remarkable structures, the more I feel a connection with the craftsmen who created them, and the more I am inspired to carry on the tradition.

Above: Architect R. Brognard Okie captured the spirit of the early Pennsylvania farmhouse, reinterpreting it with his own distinctive design vocabulary, as seen at Peaceable Farm in Bucks County.

Left: R. Brognard Okie's passion for architectural detail is apparent in this unique latch bar that he designed for an interior door at Peaceable Farm.

Following pages: View of the Delaware and Raritan Canal in Solebury, Pennsylvania.

THE HOUSES

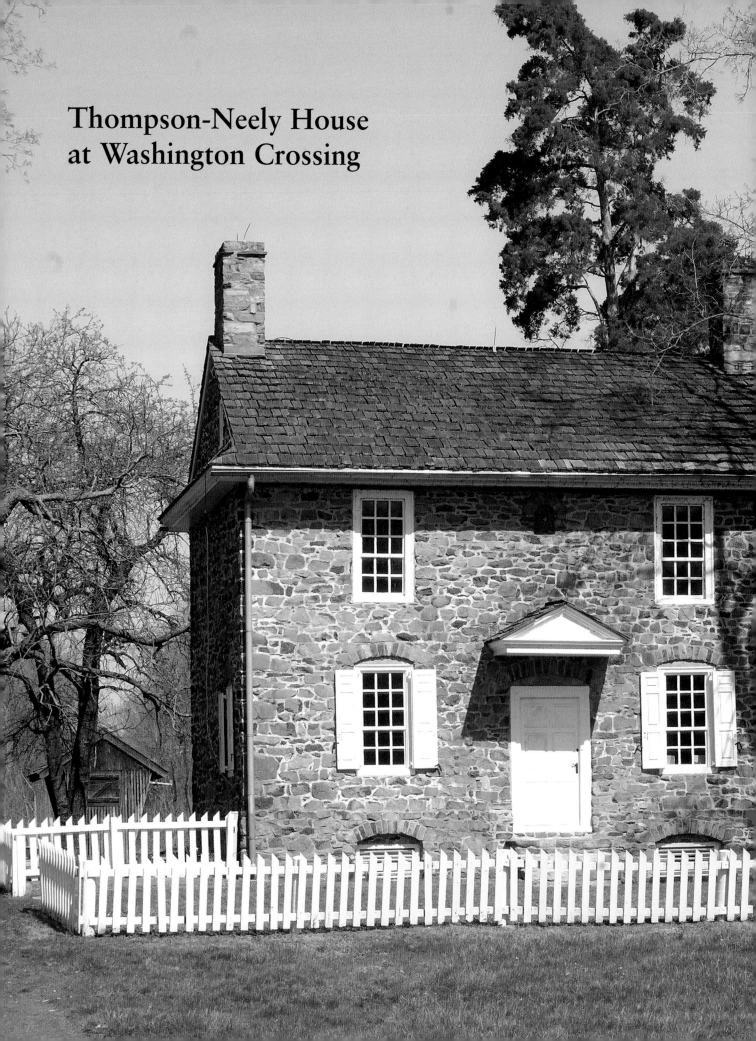

Thompson-Neely House
at Washington Crossing

Previous pages: The house is three sectioned, two-and-a-half story with the eastern end (1787–1788) double-pile. Note the shallow pediment to right, a development displacing the popularity of earlier cantilevered hoods.

Above: The "Great Room" (all-purpose), walk-in fireplace, trestle table, open-beamed

ceiling, and display mantel are accurate examples of farmhouses in the area.

Facing page: Cheeked fireplace with surrounding molding bespeaks a fine house. The ladder back chair is without style, but ubiquitous in early colonial houses. The high-backed windsor dates near the end of the eighteenth century.

A pilgrimage to Bucks County should include a drive along River Road on the west bank of the Delaware, a river that has fortuitously preserved much of its original natural beauty. Here one finds an exemplar of the much-loved Pennsylvania stone house, rising among old trees with signal dignity—the Thompson-Neely. North of Yardley, travelers enter Washington Crossing Park, which at its northern edge encompasses the Thompson-Neely House. A picture of southeastern Pennsylvania architectural vernacular at its finest, the house stands dramatically between the road and the river. An examination of its structure—an agglutination of portions built at various stages, beginning with a one-cell stone dwelling of circa 1701, with additions in 1757 and 1787—offers a comprehensive survey of a typical eighteenth-century add-on farm dwelling with outbuildings.

The earliest part of the house is thought to have been built by John Simpson (according to the Pennsylvania Historical and Museum Commission, which administers the site). Simpson, a Quaker, who lived there with his wife, owned and operated a mill, which he had built nearby, and which still stands across the street and can be visited.

When Simpson died, his wife Hannah married Robert Thompson, a Scots-Presbyterian who had been Simpson's

miller. Thompson, in 1757 butted onto the house an addition, which consisted of an upstairs and a downstairs, each level serving as one room. Soon after this, another room was added above the oldest dwelling section.

In time, the daughter of Hannah and Robert Thompson married John Neely, also a Scots-Presbyterian, who became Thompson's partner. With two families now in residence, it is believed that in this period the two successful millers and their wives built another addition (1787–1788), the double-pile east end.

These two generations, Thompson and Neely, lived together in the house, now individualized, with the younger Neelys occupying the east end; to retain independence, the Neelys cooked in the cellar and the Thompsons in the walk-in fireplace room of the earlier construction.

By the last decades of the eighteenth century, the house had become a typical add-on, mid-Atlantic-style dwelling of English derivation. Having developed from a small farm unit to a handsome dwelling, it simultaneously illustrated detailing that was both simple and more finely tuned.

During the years of the Revolution, the Thompson-Neely House played a patriotic role. It served as a hospital, possibly billeting soldiers as well, during the crisis when

The East wing, more elaborate than the other sections, offers three or four ladder-backs and a fireplace, shut probably to accommodate modern heating. The portrait is of Washington, featured because of the famous crossing down river a short distance.

Second floor cheeked fireplace with open door leading to winder to the garret.

Facing page: A hutch of simple colonial design.

Commander-in-Chief Washington, desperate after serious losses, conceived a plan to win a much-needed victory over the British forces. It was his decision, despite the snowy mid-winter of 1776, to cross the ice-strewn river through the night, then march on the Hessian regiments in Trenton. The advance on Trenton proved a splendid victory, remembered as "the turning point of the Revolution."

The key men in this account of the Thompson-Neely house were the three millers, a business whose practitioners were frequently the most financially successful settlers wherever they were found. They were essential to every settler, grinding grain and producing flax for linen. The homes of millers outclassed those of most of their neighbors, and the Thompson-Neely House is no exception, and remains to this day a prime example of the type. —MBR

The Washington Crossing Historic Park is administered by the Pennsylvania Historical and Museum Commission.

Morgan Colt House and
Studio at Phillips Mill

Above: Original wrought iron gate of design by Morgan Colt leads from main house to studio at the rear.

Left: The original Morgan Colt studio is composed of a large main room with far end wall stone chimney with small wood sided entry with loft. The building in the foreground is a modern bedroom addition.

Certain areas in the Northeast attracted artists who were profoundly influenced by the Arts and Crafts Movement of the late nineteenth century. New Hope in Bucks County was such a spot. A few Impressionist artists, including William L. Lathrop, attained prominent status in the incipient stage of the development of the New Hope area as a major art colony. Morgan Colt, after a chance meeting with William Lathrop, later became one of those locally distinguished practitioners of fine art in the early twentieth century.

Phillips Mill, the focal point of Colt's involvement with the art colony, stands about one mile north of New Hope. It began its life in 1756 with a gristmill operated by Aaron Phillips. After three generations of occupation by the Phillips family, Philadelphia Doctor George Morley Marshall purchased both the mill and several houses along with eighty acres as a summer retreat in 1896. Marshall sold the miller's house to William L. Lathrop, who then encouraged Colt to settle in the new village of artists at the ancient mill site. The young artist came to the area in the first decade of the twentieth century, buying three acres, and subsequently started an enclave of buildings that he affectionately called his "English Village." It was here, at the Inn at Phillips Mill, that he actually garnered his first commission—the designing and building of the Holmquist School for Girls.

Morgan Colt hailed from Shinnecock, New York, and was trained as an architect at Columbia University. By all standards, he was a Renaissance man with a broad array of interests and talents. His artistic endeavors included paint-

Above: Oversized overhead transverse summer beam emphasizes both the spaciousness and the delineation of the sections of the living room of the main house. More than ample light is provided by the end wall window.

Facing page: The pinnacle of original artistic expression of Morgan Colt survives at the end wall of dining room in delicately formed concrete chimney complete with genre scene at top section.

ing, sculpting, woodcarving, iron forging, and working in leather. His one particular claim to fame was that he worked in the rare medium of concrete in the buildings that he constructed.

At Phillips Mill, Colt converted an old piggery into his place of residence and later constructed a spacious studio. He also built a half dozen English-like cottages that included an unusual kennel, a forge, and a woodworking shop. This almost unique compound remains as one of the foremost preserved examples of Gothic-Tudor architecture in all of Bucks County.

Befitting his stature as a reflective and responsive artist, the two-story stone and half-timbered main house has two original rooms on the first floor that are replete with all manner of Tudor elements of architectural expression. Visitors first enter into a small entry foyer through a heavy Baroque-like front door and are led into an almost cavernous-sized living room. Oversized ceiling beams and

other exposed timbers establish the tone of the interior. Two small arch-topped fireplaces are set at either end of the room. Through other prominent wood doors the smaller-sized dining room is seen in which exposed ceiling beams are visible. Colt further affirmed his artistic gifts in rendering a diminutive fireplace in concrete and plaster with distinctive genre scenes decorating its chimney.

A stone walled courtyard with wrought iron gates forged by Colt separates the house from the studio. The studio, approached over concrete cast slab pavers, is fair-sized with plaster exterior walls. The interior is composed of one large room and a small entry. The room, with a cathedral-like ceiling, has five magnificent medieval-like trusses of graceful and exposed timbers that support the roof. Each truss rests on delicately configured concrete corbels. A spacious stone walk-in fireplace is located at the end wall. All architectural elements are set in a perfect harmony that bespeaks the joyful fascinations and aspirations of an accomplished artist. —GDH

Above: The magnificent split door in the dining room with long wrought iron strap hinges leads to the exterior. Rails and stiles of door separate various genre scenes.

Right: Similar to medieval English manor halls, Morgan Colt studio features distinctive and intricate timber framing of roof trusses. Stone chimney end wall completes panorama of artist's place of work.

Peaceable Farm

Left: The rear facade of the house at Peaceable Farm incorporates many of the design elements that are characteristic of R. Brognard Okie's work.

Above: The identification plaque at Peaceable Farm, painted in oil on board by artist David Guilmet, is inspired by Edward Hick's painting, Peaceable Kingdom.

The house at Peaceable Farm in Bucks County was built as one of a group of buildings associated with a large dairy operation established between 1930 and 1935. Designed by architect R. Brognard Okie for owners who wished to recreate the sense of an eighteenth-century English dairy farm, the buildings included a residence, barns, miscellaneous other agricultural structures, and a cottage. A house and barn existed on the site at the beginning of the project, but these were apparently removed or substantially altered by Mr. Okie. A portion of the earlier barn was incorporated in the foundation for the new barn. The Peaceable Farm property was divided from the larger farm and contains a complex of structures organized around a central courtyard, including the house, a blacksmith shop, a barn, a series of attached implement sheds, and a cottage.

Although the house was originally designed for the farm manager, it became a weekend residence for the owners while construction on the other buildings proceeded. As was customary with Okie houses, the exterior massing is broken down into components of varying heights. The result is a building with different roof-lines, perpendicular wings, and facade set-backs, creating a composition of considerable aesthetic interest and an intimate scale. Design elements that are found in many of Mr. Okie's houses include fieldstone facades laid in a rubble pattern, wall dormers, rain water gutter boxes under several of the dormer windows, wide plank window and door frames, recessed porch with wood segmental arched front, arched

Preceding pages: The original poplar woodwork in the dining room at Peaceable Farm has been stripped of its paint and refinished with a special formula of milk paint and colored waxes.

Above: The utilitarian function of the hallway in the rear wing is evident in the simplicity of its details and materials.

Above, right: The chimney breast in the living room at Peaceable Farm retains its original natural-finish white pine woodwork with a combination of rectangular and arched panels separated by a simple

mantel shelf. The curved plastered feature above the woodwork is a partial arch to support the fireplace hearth in the bedroom above.

Facing page: The ceiling in the living room is constructed of hand-planed and beaded oak joists. The white pine ceiling boards are also beaded.

Following pages: R. Brognard Okie incorporated part of the stone foundation of an early barn in his design of the new barn for Peaceable Farm.

hood above the front door, and large stone chimneys. The recessed porch at the right of the front facade provides access to the dining room, while the front door to the house is centered in the principal section of the facade.

The interior arrangement of rooms is rather informal, indicative of the building's original design as a secondary residence. The first floor of the main house incorporates a living room, dining room, kitchen, and stairway to the second floor and basement. The low rear wings incorporate a laundry room, bathroom, cloakroom, and stairway to the "hired man's room" above. The second floor of the main house has three bedrooms and a bathroom, connected by a hallway at the rear. In his introduction to *Early Domestic Architecture of Pennsylvania* by Eleanor Raymond, Mr. Okie discusses his appreciation for the early craftsmen and the influence that their work clearly had on his design approach. "Often the simpler the house the more interest-

ing the arrangement of small wall cupboards, boxed-in stairs, and so forth, and the ingenious use made of space that in the larger houses would be wasted. The interiors are, if anything, more fascinating than the exteriors and not only show what a thorough knowledge of native timber these men had and how to frame it, but are a testimony of the skill and accuracy with which the carpenters and other mechanics did their work. Their work shows that they enjoyed it."

The wonderful interior woodwork at Peaceable Farm is testimony to the fact that Mr. Okie also enjoyed his work, and excelled at it. In 1997, new owners acquired the property that had fallen into a state of serious decline, and they immediately began a painstaking and thorough restoration that is nearing completion. The barn is home to a collection of sheep, geese, guinea hens, and chickens. Mr. Okie would be pleased. —*JDM*

Tuckamony Farm

Preceding pages: A small house built for one family, then doubled with addition to the right, to accommodate a second family. Note the finely dressed stone and ribbon pointing on the later half.

Above: Slant top desk of fine quality, eighteenth century.

Right: Note the deep windowsill nurturing a cactus and many other accessories, together creating a room with appeal. All furniture is of colonial origin.

A visit to this small farmstead offers the viewer a delightfully accurate restoration of an eighteenth-century home. Today, Tuckamony Farm occupies part of an original grant (5000 acres) from William Penn. A portion of this acreage passed through a number of owners, one of whom, a Quaker, Isaac Pickering, acquired in 1742 a small piece, 157 acres. On this parcel in 1747 he built a one-cell stone house. An addition, butted against the original in 1783, was similarly of stone. Some time after this a woodshed, now made over into a modern kitchen, bath, and laundry, was joined to the addition. Since no door was included connecting these living areas, it may be inferred that two families enjoyed privacy; perhaps a child who had married or a tenant who helped with the farm work lived in the new wing. In the early twentieth century Tuckamony was bought by Forrest and Irene Crooks, who with fine discrimination restored the then neglected house to its former simple dignity.

Studying the frontal facade one can see a distinct vertical line between the original one-bay structure and the addition. A closer look at the latter reveals dressed stone with ribbon pointing, a masonry that was more formal and dressy than the original section of fieldstone with its low-ridge mortaring. Dressed stone is found occasionally, but with farmhouses it is often limited to the front wall. On the original wing a onetime door is still discernible, but altered to accommodate a corner cupboard within. In the Crooks'

Left: Four-poster bed with crocheted and quilted "furniture." The chest could have been a "wedding chest," essential for a bride.

Above: Looking down a winder, this one narrow with small treads, perhaps reflecting the small house.

restoration, the original pent was rebuilt, thus returning this early weather shelter common to the seventeenth and eighteenth centuries.

Inside, in the living room, there are original poplar floorboards, which were probably lumbered from surrounding woods, many of which in 1742 were still plaguing aspiring Bucks farmers who needed crop fields, not forests throughout the countryside. The ends of the boards taper, alternating from wide to narrow across the floor to prevent waste. The fireplaces are smaller than the walk-ins in larger homes, but one is sufficiently large for necessary cooking. It is always helpful to find a date spelled out; in the older section of the Tuckamony farmhouse, the construction year of the house, 1747, is scratched into a ceiling beam, the fourth from the fireplace near the center of the room.

Adding further interest to Tuckamony Farm, there is the foundation of another very small stone building to the southwest of the Crooks house. It is said that Peg Tuckamony, considered the last Lenni Lenape Indian to leave Bucks County, lived here, scratching out a living as a basket weaver. A few of these baskets are still in existence, now treasured as heirlooms.

In 1980, the Crooks family donated the house, barn and some land to the Heritage Conservancy, thus providing a permanent home for the individual responsible for activities on the property. The Honey Hollow Education Center, located in the Tuckamony barn, at present manages operations, which include activities in nature education, archaeology, preservation, and hosting The Bucks County Audubon Society. —MBR

The center section of the stone building dates
from the mid-eighteenth century, and the section
on the right from the 1830s. The original one-story
structure on the left, later raised to two stories,
is partially obscured by the 1990 addition.

Facing page: The spring house, built at the turn of the
nineteenth century, accommodates the spring on the
lower level and a finished room on the upper level.
The twentieth century stone bridge spans the
Cuttalossa Creek.

The Armitage House

The original parcel of land on which the Samuel
Armitage House is situated dates back to 1703, when it
was conveyed by patent from William Penn to Francis
White; it passed on to Henry Paxson several years later.

Samuel Armitage purchased the property, 200 acres in
all, from Henry Paxson in 1748. A miller, Armitage had at
least seven children and two wives, and built on his land a
house that would increase in size over the ensuing decades,
up until the 1830s. Upon his death in 1798, the house was
bequeathed to his son John, who raised nine children in it.
During this time the barn, the spring house, and the smoke
house were probably built. (The barn dates to 1786.)
Members of the Armitage family lived in the house
throughout the nineteenth century.

The oldest section of the house encompasses what is
now the dining room. The smaller, one-story structure was
most likely where the family lived while the center section
of the house was being built. There is also evidence of an
early frame addition where the current addition now
stands. The center section of the house dates to the middle
of the eighteenth century. The large center room was originally three separate rooms: a kitchen with a walk-in fireplace, a living room with a corner fireplace, and a parlor
or dining room.

The final stone addition was completed in the 1830s. A
"new" kitchen was added to the house, as was a bedroom
above it. At this time, a second story was also added to the
original structure.

Above left: The upper level room in the spring house has a small corner fireplace and exposed roof framing.

Above right: A winder stairway originally connected the three floor levels of the center section of the Armitage House. There were doors at each floor to contain heat in the rooms.

Facing page: The owner's restoration of the house in 1990 was based on extensive research and investigation, and involved replacement of missing original features such as chair rails, doors, and wrought iron hardware.

Following pages: The first floor of the center section in the Armitage House, now serving as a living room, was originally divided into three separate rooms. The exposed summer beam and floor joists in the ceiling retain evidence of the partitions that had been removed at an early date.

During the eighteenth and nineteenth centuries, the Armitage family prospered. A photograph from the 1860s reveals that the Armitage house had been clad in stucco by this date. In addition, many interior details were changed to meet the prevailing style of the day, the Victorian. Such modifications included changes in the window and door moldings.

Evidence suggests that Samuel Armitage may have been the first person to own and operate a flourmill on this property. But by the mid-nineteenth century there were at least four other flourishing grist and sawmills between here and the river along the Cuttalossa Creek alone.

In 1990 the current owners underwent a major rehabilitation and restoration of the house. Every effort was made to restore the house to its original eighteenth century condition. This included replacement of the original chair rails, display of open beam ceilings, replacement of original doors, and restoration of fireplaces in the living and dining rooms. —SP

Left; The main road for many years passed between the house and the spring house, making this location an easy spot to patronize.

Above: This large house and its setting retain about ninety percent of their historic appearance, thus providing a unique situation in the charm of authenticity which pervades.

Kockert's Tavern

Springtown village extends along a ridge in the rolling hills of the uppermost reaches of Bucks County, where fertile farm lands watered by numerous fresh water springs lured settlers who valued the land not only for its rich limey soil, but for the limestone which could be quarried or reduced to mortar in kilns. In 1764, a tired traveler riding or walking along Springtown Road would be happy to find himself approaching Kockert's Tavern, a stopover where he would find a good meal and a comfortable rest, even if he had to double up on occasion with another traveler. Innkeeper Jacob Kockert, immigrant from Rathsweiler, Germany, with his wife and father-in-law, a mason, had recently obtained the license to keep a public house of entertainment and to sell small amounts of liquor. He had bought a farm plantation, but with license in hand he now opened his doors and launched his venture; steady success was to allow him over the years to buy numerous other tracts of land. During the Revolutionary War years (1775–1781), the tavern was considered an established lodging, a favorite stopping place for soldiers headed for Washington's regiments from northern settlements. It had also an implicit raucous note—there is a tale told about the time involving a young woman who went missing, to be found a hundred years later, in 1884, a skeleton sealed up within a center chimney, and written about in the *Springtown Times* in 1891.

On Kockert's property stood a log cabin adjoined to a four-room stone house, which had been built by a former owner, English Quaker Stephen Twining. Kockert replaced

Above: The fireplace here, the earliest, offering a warm welcome to weary travelers, was built by the English Quaker owner, Stephen Twining, early in the eighteenth century.

Right: The unicorns, one-time symbols of maidenly virtue, on the wedding chest are eye-catching, stirring the imagination. The windsor chairs date 1780–1800. The sampler on the wall is dated 1819 and signed by the artist, Rachel Green.

the original log section with a stone addition butted against Twining's basic masonry. Twelve years later, in 1773, he built another stone addition to his flourishing tavern, bringing the total rooms to twelve, now an impressive way station. Four years after this improvement, at the age of 62, Kockert died, unaware that his wife Susanna was pregnant with his son, to be duly named after his father, Jacob. After contesting claims from Adam Kockert (the elder Jacob's brother) were tendered and dismissed, young Jacob was named sole heir to his father's substantial estate.

Susanna, a short time thereafter, married a Major Samuel Breckenridge who had ambitions to become an innkeeper, and soon obtained a license to do so. Until their deaths in 1797, together they ran Kockert's Tavern.

After the death of his mother and stepfather, Jacob, Jr. took over the tavern—but with the removal of the old road from directly in front of his inn to the crest of the hill, he was soon compelled to turn exclusively to farming. An energetic young man, he became a recognized leader in local politics.

For 154 years the property remained in the hands of the Kockert family; after 1915 a succession of new owners acquired ownership. The house-tavern and outbuildings, consisting of barn, spring house, smokehouse, and summer kitchen, have remained with very little alteration. Excellent examples of additive architecture, they retain about ninety percent of their historic appearance. —MBR

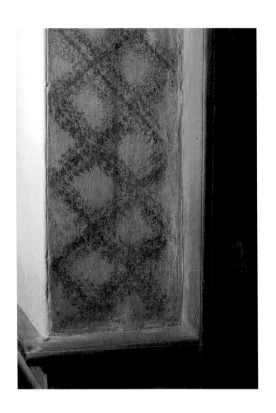

Top: Design in wall painting technique, similar to decorated walls in the Peter Wentz house.

Above: Dough table where housewives stored flour brought in from the mill. Butter scales using weights in the balance.

Right: The dining room with butternut drop-leaf trestle table. On the wall hangs a carved Netherlands cupboard with dates 1784–1806 painted by owners.

Buckingham Friends Meeting House

The Buckingham Friends Meeting House, declared a National Historic Landmark by the National Park Service of the Department of the Interior in 2003, transcends itself. Designed and built in 1768–1769 by the members of the Society of Friends, known as Quakers, this large rectangular building presents a building of dignified simplicity. Approaching the meeting house at its isolated location, a grassed eminence north of the Old York Road in Buckingham Township, the visitor immediately recognizes the building's importance. Nothing impinges on the dignity and harmony of the scene. The golden brown of the grit stone walls appears to have assimilated the warmth of the sun, the proportions strike one as harmonious, and the white trim sets off the design and placement of windows and doors.

A sharp look at the exterior absorbs the Early Georgian proportions and the stone work with narrow white mortaring of wood-burnt lime of the period. As a gesture toward decoration, the eaves run across each end as well as along the front and rear of the structure. The cornice includes a concave, plastered support, evidence of extra expense and effort in construction. This feature reflects also the overall high quality of building standards of the area—evidence of the prosperity of these settlers in Buckingham Township who were fortunate to find limestone soil under their properties. Lime in soil, as the Germans had long understood, was a superb base for agriculture; its presence was one of the important factors behind Pennsylvania's epithet, the "breadbasket" of the New World. Matthias Hutchinson, Associate Judge of Bucks County for two terms, a man of several other capacities including master mason, was responsible for the overall construction of this superb building with Edward Good of Plumstead, the chief carpenter.

The interior reflects a divergent design, a first time in the history of Quaker meeting houses, which offers the women an area equal to that of the men. So significant was this

A Quaker House of Worship that has never deviated in use since 1768. Dedicated by The Department of the Interior as a landmark, it is on the National Register of Historic Places.

Above: Area planned for women measures the same as the area for men, thus revolutionizing a biased system that all Quaker meeting houses followed. The gallery was planned so as not to isolate late-comers.

Right: The interior, featuring a Victorian stove (1874)—one of two that heated the entire building for more than a hundred years.

development that subsequently all meeting houses contemplating an enlargement or a new house of worship were told to pattern any architectural plan on that of the Buckingham Meeting.

Entering one of the six doors one becomes aware of the gallery, wide enough to furnish satisfactory overflow space at times of a full house. The main floor on the lower level is divided at approximately the middle with a partition skillfully designed with doors, shutters, and panels, which can be raised and lowered to separate the sexes at the time of monthly business sessions. The gallery can also be divided into two sections by panels arranged on cross-timbers so as to be opened or closed as need demands. Originally this was accomplished with ropes passed through pulleys, which are still visible in the ceiling. The interior woodwork including the railings in the gallery is of white cedar, the benches downstairs of poplar, a softer wood. The flooring and entry steps are of yellow pine. No woodwork has ever been painted. The fifty-foot girders throughout the framework were very heavy and cumbersome to place but, as Alice Atkinson Kirson observed in her *History of Buckingham Meeting*, "the men were giants in those days." These timbers, neatly trimmed, were hewn from logs in nearby woods. More recently, a new roof of slate, modern heating, well hidden under the side benches, and running water have completed a modernization. To the enjoyment of present attenders, especially those who recollect memories of times almost a hundred years ago, an elegant Victorian cast-iron stove (1874) in the women's side has been retained. *—MBR*

"Old Congress" of Byecroft Farm

Preceding pages: An English-derived farmhouse that avoided any serious loss of integrity over a 300 year span. The four chimneys indicate the fireplaces below, which total to seven. The ownership has not been out of one local family, a rare situation.

This venerable house of stone has grown from a dwelling first established in pioneer days as a one-cell quartzite addition to a log cabin. It has been much enlarged over the centuries. Its name, "Old Congress," originated in the early 1700s. At that time the Quaker settlers of Buckingham Township had no official house of worship, causing John Bye (son of Thomas Bye, the patentee) and John Scarborough of Buckingham to petition the mother meeting for permission to worship in the "house of Thomas Bye." This was granted. From 1702 to 1710 Buckingham Society of Friends met for worship services in the Bye

home. Later, this led to references to the house as the "old meeting" or "Congress."

In 1699, sixty-year-old Thomas Bye of Horsleydown, England, with his son, John, erected a log cabin on this site near present Lahaska. Three years later, anticipating the arrival of Thomas's wife, Margaret, and their four other children, Thomas built a stone addition to the log house. The space measured nineteen-by-nineteen feet with two entrance doors, one opposite the other, after the medieval tradition of English houses. The chimney served a fourteen-foot fireplace under a hewn oak "chimney tree." This early

The east end of the spacious living room (22 feet by 38 feet) contains a cheeked fireplace with simple molding at ceiling and chair-rail level, authentic hardware throughout, a slant top desk, and eighteenth century Chippendale chairs.

stone section with a second story added in the eighteenth century still stands. There is evidence that in about 1710 the log portion burned.

In 1732, John, second son of Thomas and Margaret, bought from his father another 600-acre grant of land acquired from the Penn heirs, to which he moved, passing the ownership of Old Congress to Nathaniel, the third son.

Nathaniel was a successful entrepreneur who made a small fortune as a fell-monger hunting beaver pelts with the Indians. In 1732 he invested in a handsome addition to the southwest wall of the original house. This two-and-a-half

story enlargement and kitchen reflects a design closer to the Georgian style than a farmhouse, but Old Congress still emerges as basically a vernacular interpretation. He added also the outbuildings necessary for a self-sufficient farm—a summer kitchen, a smokehouse, buttery, forge, barn, and stabling. The small English-type barn, still standing but separated from the subsequent large nineteenth-century bank barn adjacent to it, has been transformed into a modest, but charming stone dwelling. This addition provided three further fireplaces on the first floor and two in the rooms above. One of these, on the lower floor, is the

Left: The dining room, two steps down from living room was formerly the kitchen with a very wide fireplace opening spanned by a massive wood lintel. The open door is one of formerly two, opposite each other. Note small iron door to the bake oven.

Above: The elderly Quaker lady who created these gems of fine sewing was Rosalie Pusey Bye, who lived in Baltimore and in her old age enjoyed smoking a pipe.

kitchen walk-in and almost as large as the original, classifying this house as perhaps the only early Bucks County dwelling with two kitchens. In design, the house now embraced three sections, with the central portion raised higher than the ends, the whole containing four stone chimneys and six doors. This extension established an air of gentlemanly living which, even at this early date left the appearance of pioneer life far behind.

Nathaniel's son, Thomas II, heir to Old Congress through his older brother, Joseph, was also a prosperous man. With seven children to bring up, Thomas saw the need for further enlargement. The roof of Nathaniel's kitchen was raised, thus adding an extra bedroom, bringing the new and old wings to the same level.

Thomas III (1740–1827), only surviving son of Thomas II and heir, acquired the ancestral estate in 1786, which he enlarged and improved. After his death, the house remained as it had been, without further basic changes.

The next heir, Thomas Woolston Bye was, like his forebears, prosperous; Old Congress flourished. Of the four sons born to Thomas Woolston, only one grew to maturity, inheriting the estate. This was John Hart Bye, who also prospered. Nonetheless, during the next three generations Old Congress suffered gradual neglect. Ambitious young men began to leave the farms. It was not until the 1930s and 40s that a return to the country became highly desirable.

Old Congress, fortunately still owned by descendants, was acquired in 1930 by Arthur Edwin Bye of the tenth generation. He modernized the homestead with an appropriate kitchen wing, central heat and water, and other improvements including the transformation of the stone wagon house into a home for himself. In 1981, the entire Byecroft Farm was placed on the National Register for Historic Places under the Department of the Interior. —*MBR*

The Eight-Square Schoolhouse

Left: This small, charming building with the bridge in the right background warms the heart; the setting recalls happy schooldays and peace. Three of the eight walls are pictured. Large "quoins" were used in construction of the corners.

Above: The close-up suggests that even small corner stones can do the job.

Still sits the schoolhouse by the road,
A ragged beggar sunning;
Around it still the sumacs grow
And blackberry vines a-running.
—Anonymous

The date was October 1773. The parents around Oxford Valley, Bucks County, were complaining about the inadequacy of their children's schoolhouse. A committee, consisting of a small number of local farmers and artisans in charge of planning for a new building, came forward with a revolutionary proposal offered by one of the members, Moses Moon: a new schoolhouse should be octagonal in design. The suggestion was approved.

The local fathers moved quickly. Two days later they met again with horses and wagons to select stone, in those days the cheapest and best way to build. In less than a year they had erected a one-room eight-square schoolhouse which immediately became a popular choice for school buildings throughout the area. So successful was this experiment that more than one hundred octagonal schoolhouses were built in the Delaware Valley before 1840.

The Wrightstown Octagonal School, pictured here, was patterned after the one in Oxford Valley. Like all others of similar design it solved some of the major problems of earlier schoolhouses built in rectangular form. It stands today among only a few that have survived from that innovative period, when eight-square one-room schools were considered highly desirable and were later lovingly cared for over the years by former attenders sensitive to the importance of this now rare educational artifact.

Thus, the octagonal design carried out successfully in 1773, came on the scene sixty-one years before the system of public schooling had become the responsibility of taxpayers, by a bill passed by the Pennsylvania Congress in 1834. The proposal made that October evening was

Above: Display table with cabinet.

Facing page: The small stove with the towering stack has a modern flair in its simplicity.

straightforward and realistically within the construction abilities of local parents throughout the southeastern area of Pennsylvania and New Jersey. The fabric of these little schoolhouses could be fieldstone or wood with a window installed in each of the seven walls, not counting the doorway. The exact shape and size of these small buildings, to which elementary students came on foot or horse, proved

eminently successful. Environmental advantages were clear; the alleviation of the darkness in corners, improved heating by a wood-stove located in the center of the room with the children gathered in widening circles around and the quality of light as a result of doubling the previous standard number of windows. None of the octagonal schools deviated very far from this example. These early private schools operated as independent, non-sectarian institutions supported by the families influential in their construction.

What was the precedent that inspired the choice of these octagonally shaped schoolhouses? This is the sixty-four-dollar question that has baffled researchers. Other eight-sided buildings, such as churches, meeting houses, windmills, and garden houses were known, but rarely used in the New World. Quakers and Lutherans were leading educational reformers, but they have never been linked with the design for the schoolhouses in question.

Architectural historian Robert W. Craig proposes that the octagonal schoolhouses of America were inspired by the "garden houses" of similar design prevalent in British landscape planning of the eighteenth century. This development had grown out of a fascination with classical pavilions and temples, which appealed to estate and plantation owners in both England and America. Thomas Jefferson used the design for his home; George Washington had actually converted one of his four garden houses to a schoolhouse.

Moses Moon, a member of the original committee and sponsor of the original design was literate and interested in education and architecture. He with his father, both horticulturalists as well as farmers, sold garden seedlings and could easily have been aware of these unusual eight-square buildings as described in some of the landscape-architecture books that the father, James Moon, is known to have brought back from Philadelphia to his library.

This suggestion as to the precedent of octagonal schoolhouses may well be correct, but their popularity derived from other sources. They were practical; they satisfied the needs of teachers and children, their ambience lingering as a happy experience in the memories of most graduates. Eight-square schoolhouses endured for seventy-eight years, the last one having been erected in 1851. At this time, New England designers of schools, ignorant of the eight-square schoolhouse form and lacking an effective spokesman, returned to rectangularity. Children were once more to sit behind desks in rows.

In the history of education the place of the octagonal schoolhouse is now designated as the first radical reform in school design in the United States, a development that considered environmental factors as well as learning. Perhaps it is significant to remember that the founders of this movement were Bucks County settlers already geared to reform and experiment. —MBR

The Prickett House

Preceding pages: English boxwood lines the walk leading to
the entrance of modest Greek
revival spirit. The plan within
is Georgian, designated as a
two-thirds or side-hall design.
The two sections were built at
the same time, making a simple but successful element of
visual interest.

Right; Brass moon face of an
all-original tall case clock of
local importance. Clock-
maker was Solomon Parke of
Newtown, Pennsylvania, who
later worked in Philadelphia
(1797–1820).

Facing page: Dining room with
high-backed windsor chair, a
brass-faced grandfather clock, and
samplers over an eighteenth-century chest of drawers. The spoon-
holder offers a decorative footnote
in this sunny corner.

The Prickett House presents a superb illustration of how many people in Bucks County lived in the hoary days of almost two hundred years ago. The approach to the house consists of a double line of boxwood that shields the path leading to the front entrance, with a portico supported by pillars and pilasters under a gently sloping roof. This entrance door, reduced at some undesignated time from two doors to one large door, gives a hint of the Greek Revival mode emerging out of the more prominent Georgian still dominant within the house. The date of the Prickett house is set, although not documented anywhere, for circa 1825. The plan is Georgian, of the two-thirds or side-hall subtype, in which the door opens into a hall with two rooms to one side. In the case of this house a smaller stone wing, built at the same time, provides more down-stairs living space. A second wing, wood frame and added much later, provides a kitchen and utilities area.

Entering through the front door, one immediately senses perfection. The colors are subtle. The period furniture is settled around the rooms in an inviting manner. And the curtains are appropriately modest. The thought comes to the visitor that in such a dwelling many established Bucks County residents could preserve their treasured heirlooms,

their documents, artifacts, and pictures, and, best of all, practice a distinguished way of life, which is now to most only a memory. Upstairs one finds the same taste and elegance with further evidence of the Greek Revival in an eared fire mantle in one of bedrooms.

A word or two may bring understanding of the Greek Revival style and its prominence after the Revolutionary War, a style that expressed the Americans' new freedom and independence. Americans were consciously seeking ways to show satisfaction in their newly won independence, and when archaeologists and architects began to report the beauty and dignity of ancient Greek architecture they had found in Athens and Rome, the thrust toward this handsome style of architecture took hold. It was spread by pattern books and carpenter's guides from Maine to the Gulf Coast to Texas and throughout the Midwest, with important architects such as Benjamin H. Latrobe, Alexander Jackson Davis, and others eager to design in this newly adapted Greek approach. It was used in all types of construction, beginning with public buildings, such as the Bank of the United States (1818) and other important edifices in Philadelphia, to be soon followed elsewhere, widely so in the design of houses.

A fine set of windsor chairs surround a turned leg trestle table lighted with an old chandelier of many lights. The beamed ceiling of this onetime kitchen was once plastered.

A painted linen cabinet with molding and straight feet accompanied by a windsor chair, dated late eighteenth century.

Facing page: Wall of the old kitchen, now foil for decorative objects, such as the pewter plate and two mugs.

A further source of interest in the Prickett heritage is a dignified stone barn, the interior of which has been adapted from a sturdy, awesome open space to nine rooms of remarkably fine antique furniture and decorative objects, authenticated, documented and guaranteed , on display for the collector. The garden areas around the house and barn are as carefully thought out as the house and barn. Close to the front door stands a charming stone well house, at a spot on which a former owner had erected a steel tower. The removal of this in exchange for the present diminutive structure leaves the viewer with the conviction that all is in order at the Prickett domain; there is nothing here to affront the eye, nor disturb the serenity of the soul. —*MBR*

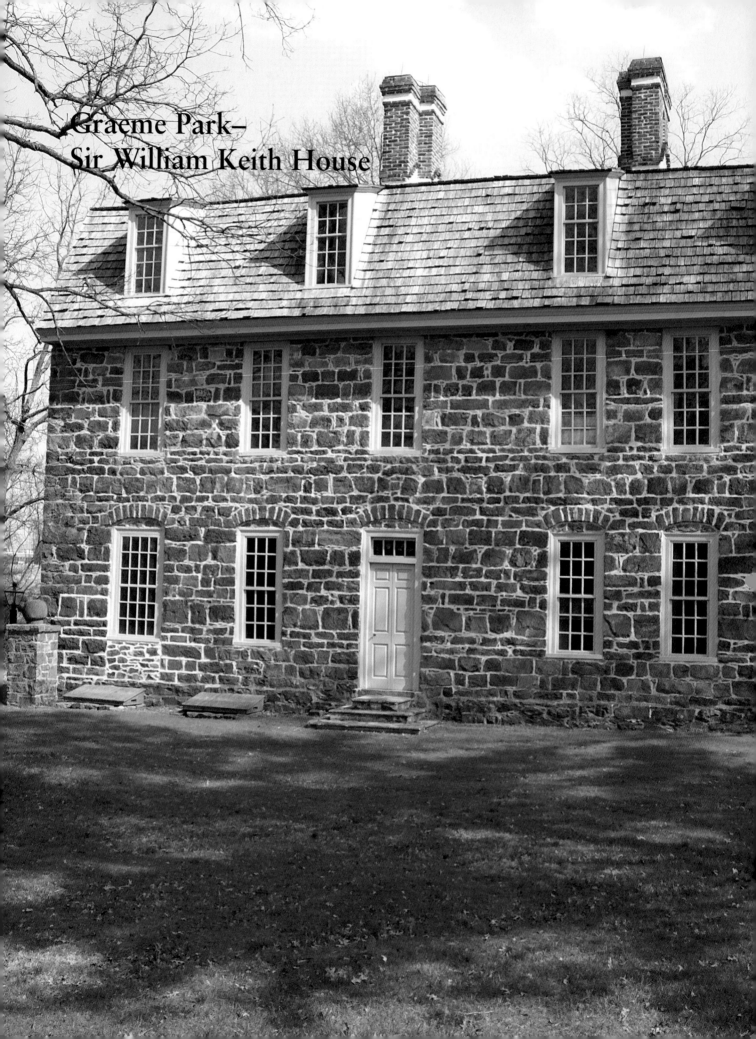

Graeme Park–
Sir William Keith House

Left: An exterior that belies the beauty and style of High Georgian within. An inspection of the masonry, however, convinces one that the mason cared about quality. The small building to the right is a reconstructed kitchen where lavish foods were turned out.

Above: Detail of one of the high, narrow outer doors. The mansion appears to be almost a fortress.

He was wont to ride to church,
over the special road built for him,
in his emblazoned coach, with four horses,
liveried footmen, and outriders.
—from Hugh Morrison's
Early American *Architecture*

When approaching the Keith House in Horsham Township, seventeen miles from Philadelphia, one is intrigued, if not puzzled, to come upon this imposing and dignified brownstone dwelling which conjures up a medieval retreat. The builder, Sir William Keith (1669–1749), appointed by William Penn as Provincial Governor of the province of Pennsylvania in 1717, had lived for some years in Philadelphia, then the most sophisticated and important city in the New World. Desiring a country place to live in during the hot months, Keith bought 1200 acres (the house now sits on 42 acres) on which to build a summer home in the "wilderness," now Montgomery Township. For Keith's benefit, the road from Philadelphia was improved and a new approach built to reach his isolated retreat. He named it "Fountain Low." Keith, scion of an ancient Scottish family, was in part unpre-

Top: Sturdy, yet beautiful in the Georgian manner, beautiful railings give confidence to young and old.

Above: The garret, reserved for children's nursery and sleeping quarters.

Facing page: The finely detailed chimney breast incorporates a fireplace with tile hearth and marble surround, mantel shelf, dog-eared frame, broken pediment, and dentil cornice.

tentious, asserting that he did not wish anything "ornamental." A Scotsman, he styled his country home in denial of the elaborate architectural developments that were, at that time, emerging in the English early-Georgian period.

On December 12, 1721, Keith hired mason John Kirk to construct a two-and-a- half-story stone house with tall, narrow doors and windows, and a simple cornice. The plan and the gambrel roof followed the Swedish tradition. The roof, high atop the extended walls (to accommodate 14-foot-high ceilings characteristic of summerhouses), and the shutterless, nine-over-nine windows resulted in stark severity. Successfully approximating the look of dressed stone the coursed ashlar masonry walls were carefully pointed. Service quarters and domestic offices were planned for separate buildings.

Sir William and his family lived in this summer mansion in noteworthy fashion. He entertained prodigally, indifferent to what the future might bring. In 1726, however, continuing to display loyalist leanings, he fell out of favor with Penn, was relieved of his governorship, and retired to his summer edifice. Sometime later he sailed for England. Unhappily, he failed to raise the funds necessary to clear debts he had incurred or to pay for transporting his family back to England. Sentenced to debtor's prison, he died in 1749.

In 1739 Philadelphia physician Dr. Thomas Graeme purchased Fountain Low. With a bow to the Scottish architect James Gibbs, he began to remodel the interior in the "advanced" Georgian style which had become fashionable. Step by step, Graeme transformed the decor on both levels. He added paneling, door enframements, mantelpieces, and fireplace surrounds with tiles edging the fireplaces, rarely appearing in such an early house. The four walls of the east drawing room, an area twenty feet square, are paneled from floor to ceiling. The room features a fireplace with overmantel, its panel framed by an eared architrave below a broken pediment and flanked by two pedimented doors. One of these is false, included solely to carry out the balance mandatory to a Georgian interpretation.

After Thomas Graeme's death in 1772 a series of owners followed, including the Penrose family, who constructed a smaller stone house as residence and the bank barn, now the visitors' center. Welsh and Margaret Strawbridge became the last private owners in 1922. In 1958 they gave the remaining forty-two acres and mansion to the Commonwealth of Pennsylvania. —*MBR*

Graeme Park–Sir William Keith House is administered by the Pennsylvania Historical and Museum Commission with the support of The Friends of Graeme Park.

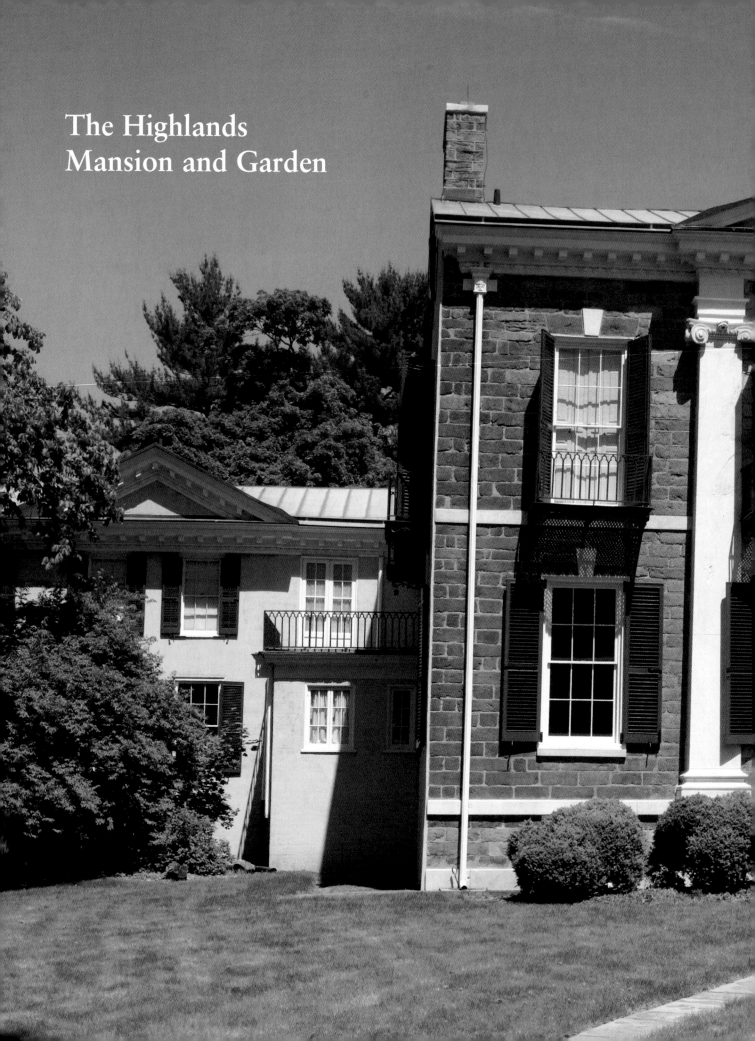

The Highlands
Mansion and Garden

Anthony Morris (1766–1860)—politician and merchant—may not have secured lasting material wealth (he was bankrupt by 1809), but the grand manor that he created at The Highlands in Fort Washington remains as an enduring tribute to his vision of architectural splendor. Morris started to build his magnificent pastoral residence in June 1795. The house, which included diverse late Georgian and early Federal style embellishments, was completed six years later. The account books that he laboriously maintained cite innumerable artisans and craftsmen whom he hired and diverse funds that were needed for varied construction projects. The Philadelphia and Lancaster architect "T. Matlack" (likely Timothy Matlack) designed the manor house. Morris also built an imposing contemporary stone barn that first greets visitors who come to The Highlands. Its plan is unique in Pennsylvania.

Faced with devastating financial problems, Morris was forced to sell his beloved mansion house and 200 acres of land to Daniel Hitner in 1808. George Sheaff in 1813 bought The Highlands and more than 300 acres from Hitner. It was during the Sheaff family occupancy, which lasted more than a century, that numerous improvements were made to the mansion and to the landscape.

Sheaff, a wine merchant, cultivated a variety of grapes and established the "Pleasure Ground," the garden to the east of the house, by the 1840s. Various lengths of

Left: A prominent armillary sphere overlooks the "Pleasure Grounds" or garden to the east of the mansion established by George Sheaff in the first half of the nineteenth century. The gardener's cottage with crenellated walls occupies the northeast corner.

Above: Two arbors designed by William Eyre in 1918 usher visitors to different sections of the garden. Shown is the north arbor that is adorned by roses held in place by cedar posts and cross pieces.

substantial stone wall delineate much of the garden grounds. The crenellated north stone wall and the Gardner's Stone Cottage at the northeast corner date from this era. Here Morris originally planted rye.

Succeeding the long tenure of the Sheaff family, the property passed into the fastidious hands of Miss Caroline Sinkler in 1917. Undaunted by the deteriorating condition of both the house and gardens, Sinkler extensively restored them. Evincing a sensitive appreciation of ancient refinements, she added an exedra—an outdoor "room" with seats for conversation. At The Highlands, it is denoted by a pink semi-circular stone wall and accented with a stone pedestal topped with an urn-like vessel. The exedra appears beyond the south stone wall sections that she installed about 1920. In 1918, Sinkler created a Lord and Burnham greenhouse outside the east wall. Intersecting grass aisles divide the majority of the garden into quadrants—a boxwood parterre appears in the northwest section. The aisles had already been established during Sheaff's ownership. An armillary sphere adorns the center of the parterre garden, and is a miniature representation of the earth used through the centuries by those preoccupied with things celestial.

Emily Sinkler Roosevelt, the niece of Miss Sinkler, and her husband Nicholas acquired The Highlands, then reduced to 44 acres, in 1941. Aware of the historical treasure they possessed, the Roosevelts transferred the property to the Commonwealth of Pennsylvania in 1957. Mrs. Roosevelt died in 1970 and the state thereafter began their comprehensive restoration and rehabilitation efforts at the property in 1975. Significant vestiges of all The Highlands' occupants through the past two centuries can still be seen at this stately manor. —*GDH*

Pennsbury Manor

Previous pages: This reconstructed manor house on the Delaware River, originally planned and specified by William Penn, founder of Pennsylvania, has proven very successful. Both plan and detail reflect the late seventeenth century.

Right: The main staircase, sturdy and handsome in its design, offers confidence and pleasure in its use.

Facing page: Tiled fireplace, a very early tall case clock, a Jacobean cupboard on elongated and spiraled legs are appropriate to the period in style and the social standing of William Penn. The furniture throughout the house justly displays the trappings of wealth.

Oh how sweet, is the quiet of these parts, freed from the anxious and troublesome solicitations, hurries and perplexities of woeful Europe.

—William Penn

It is serendipitous that we have the opportunity to visit Pennsbury Manor, the reconstructed manorial home of William Penn (1644–1718), a statesman to whom anyone proud of our democratic culture owes a great debt. A son of wealth and privilege, William Penn offered the persecuted of England and the continent of Europe a chance to live without unfair taxation and religious oppression. He had intelligence, wisdom, a sense of social responsibility, and great courage. Pennsbury Manor as a memorial sanctuary, designed and built in the late seventeenth century by William Penn, the distinguished Quaker founder of Pennsylvania, is an inspiration.

Having persuaded King Charles to offer him territory in the New World to cover a debt owed by the king to William's deceased father, Sir William Penn, the young Penn was encouraged to work out his dream of a new colony based on love and integrity, a "Holy Experiment." In 1672, he married Gulielma Maria Springett, a wealthy daughter of a Quaker family, adding to the inherited largesse from his father. He also acquired title to a parcel of land in New Jersey, bordering the territory that was to become Pennsylvania. Penn now combined his Quaker principles, his monetary assets, and his social position, in the venture that he wished to undertake.

During the next year, Penn planned and promoted his colony. He delegated agents to carry out his wishes and wrote, in consultation with political theorists, a "Frame of Government," extending freedom of worship to persons of all Christian persuasions and guaranteeing trial by jury to all citizens in his new colony. In 1682, Penn made his first trip to Pennsylvania, where he designated the first three counties,

Above: The Jacobean furniture, reflecting a style popular during the reign of James (1603–1625) reflects Penn's wealthy background. Muted colors throughout create harmony.

Facing page: The Great Hall. The furniture here continues the Jacobean expression; with light from the graceful chandelier important guests were treated to a splendid dinner.

Bucks, Chester, and Philadelphia. Even before leaving England he had drawn up a plan for Philadelphia, where he would establish his Frame of Government giving form to his Holy Experiment. As well he had entrusted to his cousin William Markham the choice of a site in the countryside suitable for a manor house and grounds. In response to this request, Markham chose an 8,000-acre, forested parcel in Bucks County, situated on the Delaware River. Through agents and Penn's own endeavors, a bevy of workers, gardeners, skilled stone masons, bricklayers, joiners, carpenters, glassmakers, and blacksmiths originating from England or the neighborhood had been hired to develop his estate. Instructions, spelled out carefully in his own hand, guaranteed a manor worthy of a man who was a statesman who gained world recognition, who had ideals, character, courage, and ability to forge his ideals into reality. He wrote to a friend, "God, that has given it me through many difficulties will, I believe, bless and make it the seed of a Nation ... " This was written in 1681, ninety-five years before the "Declaration of Independence" in Penn's

Philadelphia. His "Holy Experiment" had been the seed from which a great Nation had been born.

That Pennsbury was neglected after Penn's death was partly because of its distance from Philadelphia, comfortably accessible only by boat, requiring a five-hour trip. The sons, John and Thomas, were not interested. Gradually, it fell into ruins and was demolished. In the 1930s, architect R. Brognard Okie was retained by the Commonwealth of Pennsylvania to design the reconstruction of Pennsbury Manor, based on William Penn's own writings, English architectural precedent, and archeological excavations that had revealed foundation walls for the original house measuring forty feet wide by sixty feet long. The construction work required two years, and the project was completed in 1939. —MBR

Pennsbury Manor is administered by the Pennsylvania Historical and Museum Commision.

Caleb Pusey House

Above: The later 1690s addition is shown with the secondary front facade entrance door and single window and arched wall opening that lead to area where fire was tended.

Left: Humbleness and quaintness equally permeate the air about this miracle survival vernacular cottage first constructed by Caleb Pusey in the 1680s.

Defying all odds, through more than three centuries of exposure to the extremes of weather and other modifying agents, the Caleb Pusey house has survived as one of the earliest and greatest late-seventeenth-century architectural jewels in the state of Pennsylvania. The structure is so ancient-looking and quaint, one would think that the building was transported directly to America from a remote country road of sixteenth-century England. For an antiquated appearance, the Pusey house simply has no rivals.

Caleb Pusey, born in 1651 in Berkshire England, bought 250 acres from William Penn in 1681. The following year he came to America and settled in Upland. Documentation provided by the owners indicates that Pusey may have built the house in 1683.

The Pusey house retains most of it original appearance with the exception that the earlier of the two house sections had its original very steep medieval-like gable roof altered to a stylish and more efficient gambrel style sometime after about 1750. Two one-room sections comprise the Pusey house. Stone construction is seen on the entire exterior except for brick above the eave level at the east-end wall and certain sections of the later addition. Each house section is one story in height with a loft or garret above. The older eastern section, a strikingly diminutive 24 feet by 18 feet, has a large 12-foot walk-in cooking fireplace at its west-end wall. Reminiscent of so many early English houses, the chimney is almost centered on the roof. A prominent beehive bake oven that extends into the west house section is combined with a brick kettle stand with fire chamber beneath. Overhead beams are visible and reproduction casement windows adorn the front (or south) wall at either side of the centered door.

The western section contains an arched opening on the front wall to build and stoke a fire in the chamber under the kettle stand. As originally seen in the east house section, the roof on the western section is gable-ended. With its western

Left: Original 1680s section with massive restored walk-in fireplace with lintel and overhead ceiling joists render primitive-like conditions of more than three centuries ago. Brick area at right side of fireplace is bake oven at top and wood storage vault below.

Above: In the earliest times, a stark atmosphere was seen with white washed walls and sparsely furnished conditions of rooms.

Following pages: Early English-style furniture was likely exclusively seen in the last two decades of the seventeenth century in the Pusey house.

section constructed before the start of the eighteenth century, the Pusey house is distinguished as one of the extreme rarities in all of Pennsylvania in that both its sections were built prior to 1700.

An 1870s photograph graphically displays the house in very dilapidated condition. However, the ancient house, although occupied for most of the nineteenth century and beyond, never had modern amenities and its basic original structure has been miraculously maintained. However, some of the original interior fabric related to fireplace, bake oven, and kettle stand had been removed as part of an early alteration. Then, through the first half of the twentieth century, many half-hearted efforts to stabilize the house were made. Later, famed local architect G. Edwin Brumbaugh remarked that if something was not done to save the house, Pennsylvania's last remaining home with a documented association with William Penn would be nothing more than rubble. In August 1960 The Friends of the Caleb Pusey House, Inc. was formed. Restoration began two years later following extensive archeological and architectural investigations. —GDH

House Designed
by Architect
G. Edwin Brumbaugh

Designed in 1937 by G. Edwin Brumbaugh, this Delaware Valley house is an excellent example of the architect's scholarly approach to designing new buildings based on the architectural forms and traditions of the eighteenth century. Throughout his career Mr. Brumbaugh undertook serious study, not only of early buildings, but also of the furniture and decorative arts that were associated with the time periods of these buildings, and the historical developments that place them in context.

Based on his thorough knowledge of the way buildings were built in the eighteenth and early nineteenth centuries, and of the methods for fashioning and assembling individual materials to create a structure, Mr. Brumbaugh was highly respected as both a restorer and a designer. This residence reflects the architect's understanding of how and why early houses grew and evolved over time, creating the additive character that reflects their long history. He had a fondness for building in stone, and worked closely with the masons to achieve the historically correct pattern and texture of the walls. The window and door frames were made as they would have been made in the eighteenth century, for to do it any other way would have compromised the authenticity that was Mr. Brumbaugh's goal.

In his design of interior spaces and details, historical precedent was always a primary consideration with matters of room dimensions, proportion and specific woodwork configuration. The owners of this house recall long discussions with the architect about his particular source of inspiration for each of the mantelpieces and other woodwork features, as well as for the appropriate historic paint color schemes. The building was expanded in 1967 with conversion of an existing garage to a "keeping room" designed by Mr. Brumbaugh. Incorporated in the

Previous pages: G. Edwin Brumbaugh's residential designs reflect the incremental development of Pennsylvania farmhouses over time. Extensive knowledge of eighteenth and early nineteenth century vernacular architecture is evident.

Above: A two-level library wing, designed by architect John Milner, was added to the original Brumbaugh residence in 1990. The opening in the second floor provides natural light for the reading table. All of the woodwork is grain-painted, and the yellow pine flooring is composed of antique material.

Above: Mr. Brumbaugh incorporated a bay window in the dining room to provide an expansive view of the garden. Corner cupboards, the design for which was based on late-eighteenth-century precedent, flank the large window.

Facing page: In his design of the den, Mr. Brumbaugh utilized architectural elements often found in early vernacular houses, including exposed ceiling joists, plaster walls with chair rails, a molded wood mantelpiece and random-width wood flooring.

large walk-in fireplace was a beehive bake oven, the dome of which projected to the exterior and was covered by a porch, consistent with historical precedent. The asymmetrical configuration of the wood ceilings beams was designed by the architect as a rational solution to the physical constraints imposed by working with the old garage. It was, as he explained, "how they would have done it." A new stone and wood frame carriage house and barn was also added, forming a rear service courtyard.

In 1981, a new pavilion building designed by architect John Milner was constructed in the garden adjacent to the swimming pool, and in 1990, a new library wing, also designed by John Milner, was added to the main house.

Above: The rear porch provides cover for the keeping room entrance door and weather protection for the dome of the beehive bake oven that projects from the back of the large cooking fireplace. The oven has a "squirrel-tail" flue above the dome to direct smoke to the fireplace chimney flue.

Right: The keeping room is indicative of G. Edwin Brumbaugh's desire to achieve historical accuracy in creating a new room that would be faithful to architectural precedent of the mid-eighteenth century. The dimensions of the fireplace, position of the bake oven opening at the rear of the fireplace, and the size and configuration of the summer beam and ceiling joists are all details that could have been incorporated in early Delaware Valley houses.

Above: The garden and swimming pool pavilion, designed by architect John Milner, accommodates changing rooms, an octagonal parlor with a loft above, and a small kitchen. The design complements, but contrasts with, the original Brumbaugh house.

Facing page: The entrance hall, with antique brick floor, plaster walls and eighteenth century style woodwork, leads to the parlor and changing rooms. The "interior" window borrows light for the parlor from the wide entrance doorway.

Above: The loft above the parlor features a wood slat railing inspired by the Germanic tradition as seen in the Old Lutheran Church in Trappe, Montgomery County, and in the Moravian buildings in Bethlehem, Pennsylvania, and elsewhere.

Right: The loft is accessible from the parlor by means of a wood ladder.

Facing page: The octagonal parlor features a fireplace with a grain-painted chimney breast and other woodwork inspired by eighteenth-century precedent including the molded wood cornice, stepped chair rail, and door and window trim. The wood floor is painted in a checkerboard pattern.

Following pages: Architect John Milner's design of this house was inspired by the proportions, materials and details found in the late colonial architecture of southeastern Pennsylvania.

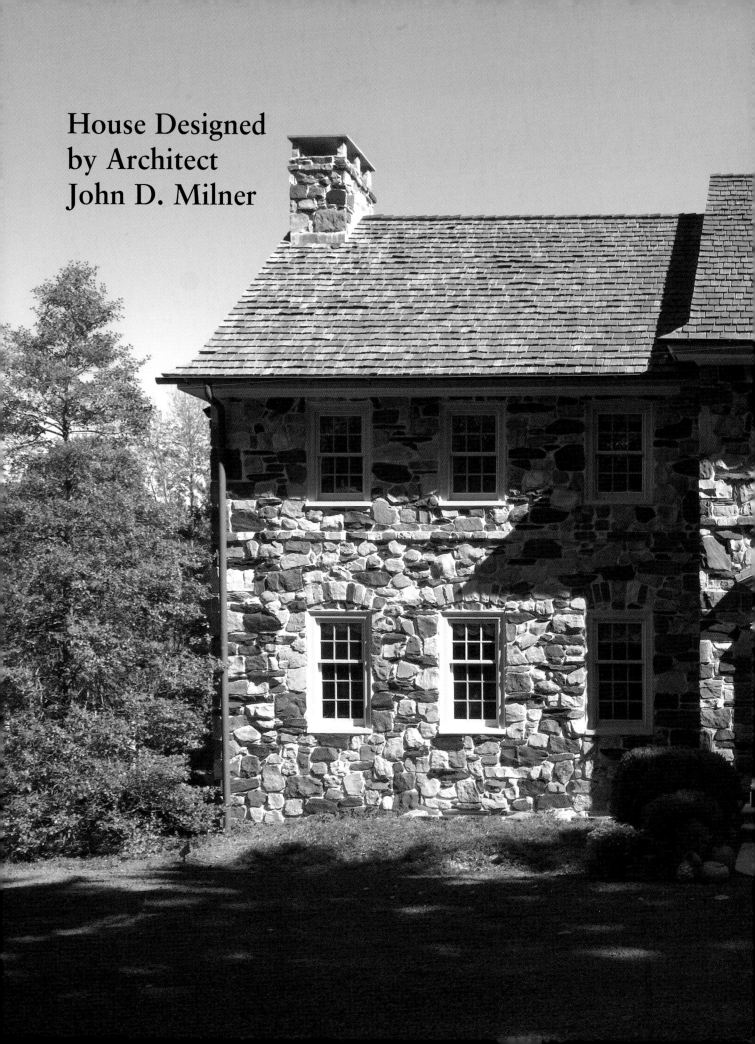

House Designed
by Architect
John D. Milner

Previous pages: John Milner's design was inspired by the proportions, materials, and details found in the late colonial architecture of southeastern Pennsylvania.

Facing page: Woodwork in the living room is an assembly of architectural components that are characteristic of fine houses of the period including wall paneling, molded wood cornices, window seats, and chair rails.

Above: The antique chimney breast, with a tabernacle frame over the fireplace mantelpiece, was acquired to serve as a focal point for the living room.

Following pages: Milner's design of the keeping room woodwork, built of antique long-leaf yellow pine boards sawn from old barn beams, was influenced by early eighteenth century precedent in the Delaware Valley. The pierced wood screens above the cabinet doors functioned historically as ventilation devices for closets.

Pages 122–123: The dining room with its paneled fireplace wall, shell cupboards, paneled wainscot, and painted floor cloth provides an appropriate setting for the owners' collection of fine American furniture and decorative arts.

Built in the late 1980s, this house was designed by architect John Milner for owners with a passion for collecting fine furniture and decorative arts. The building is an expression of the proportions, materials, and fine detailing of late-colonial-period houses in southeastern Pennsylvania. John Milner's basic concept was to create a hierarchy of form and detail in the exterior facades and the interior spaces.

In keeping with the tradition of incremental expansion of early houses over time, the building is a composition of three discrete elements. The principal and most formal section of the front facade features a doorway with an arched fanlight transom and carved wood surround, set to the left consistent with a side hall floor plan typical of the late colonial and early Federal period. A less formal wing to the left is recessed from the plane of the principal facade, as a later addition might have deferred to the original building. The exterior walls of these two elements are constructed of fieldstone, laid in a random rubble pattern, with segmental arches over the first floor windows and horizontal belt courses under the second floor windows. The fieldstone was selected from five different sources in order to achieve the desired color palate. The proportions and details of the door surround, window frames and sash, and the molded wood cornices are based on historical precedent. The rear wing, placed in a position usually reserved for utilitarian functions, is clad in wood siding.

John Milner's design of the interior spaces and decorative woodwork is an extension of the hierarchy of the facades. The formal hallway, with a stair to the second floor, extends the full depth of the principal section and opens to the garden. The living room to the right of the hallway has a centered fireplace with a formal mantel and tabernacle frame above. The woodwork of the chimney breast is an antique element, acquired by the architect for his clients. The balance of the woodwork in the room was designed to complement that period piece. The dining room, to the left of the hallway, features a paneled chimney breast with flanking arched cupboards and a paneled wainscot. The ceilings of the cupboards are composed of plaster shells in the form of half-domes. The hand-planed yellow pine flooring in the hallway, living room, and dining room was salvaged from a late-eighteenth-century house that had been demolished. The rear wing accommodates the kitchen, practically designed for contemporary living and opening to the garden, and the keeping room with exuberant heart pine woodwork based on early-eighteenth-century precedent. Antique hand hewn oak beams form the ceiling of the keeping room. The floors in the kitchen and keeping room are composed of antique paving bricks. The second floor incorporates four bedrooms, each with woodwork ranging from formal in the principal section to informal in the rear wing.

The Schilling Residence, "Florin"

Preceding pages: Architect R. Brognard Okie's characteristic "style" is clearly illustrated in the front facade of the Schilling Residence.

Above: Mr. Okie often combined square and arched raised panels in his designs of chimney breast woodwork. The curved fireplace hearth is another of the architect's personal trademarks, as is the sloping fireplace screen.

Right: Mr. Okie's houses always seem to be comfortable in their surroundings because the connection between building and landscape has been carefully considered. The carriage house in the left foreground was designed by architect John Milner.

The Montgomery County house known as "Florin" was built between 1940 and 1942 for Charles and Helen Schilling. The Schillings were serious collectors of fine American antiques, and their superb residence, designed by architect Richardson Brognard Okie, was the ideal repository for their acquisitions. Florin is a remarkably intact example of Mr. Okie's twentieth century revival and interpretation of eighteenth- and early- nineteenth-century residential architecture in the Delaware Valley. This interpretation is highly personal and unique, and his work has had a lasting impact on residential design in the region for the past six decades.

The two-and-one-half-story building, with exterior walls of rubble pattern fieldstone and beaded wood siding, incorporates many of the exterior and interior details that are associated with Mr. Okie. His design captures the additive character of early houses that had been incrementally expanded over time as owners became more prosperous. In what appears to be a conscious effort to reduce the scale of the building's exterior mass on the front facade, he introduced "wall dormers," second floor windows that are shared by the vertical plane of the wall and the sloping plane of the roof. Since these dormers interrupted the eave of the roof, the architect created a system of multiple gutters and downspouts to conduct rainwater from the roof to the ground. As is the case in many of Mr. Okie's houses, the front door is discretely tucked under a modest shed-roof porch.

The interior floor plan arrangement and abundant woodwork details found at Florin are trademarks of

Above: The diminutive scale of the moldings on this bedroom fireplace woodwork is representative of Mr. Okie's personal interpretation of eighteenth and early nineteenth century design traditions.

Right: Schilling House living room with wood paneled fireplace wall.

R. Brognard Okie's design approach. The entrance hall extends the full depth of the house, contains the stairway to the second floor, and provides access to the living room, dining room, and library. The paneled fireplace wall of the living room incorporates round arched openings leading to shallow alcoves, one containing a door to the exterior. Although Mr. Okie intended that most of the interior woodwork in his houses be painted, he often designed one room, such as the library at Florin, in natural wood. The creation of vistas through multiple interior spaces is a characteristic of the architect's work, the second floor hallway being an excellent example. Here one looks through a series of rectangular, segmental arched and round arched doorways from a narrow hall through the stair hall to a bedroom beyond.

When the current owners acquired Florin in 1998, the house was in its original condition and had never been modified since completion for the Schillings in 1942. Great care was taken to preserve and restore the exterior and interior details, including the hand-planed wide-board hemlock flooring. To fulfill the requirements of contemporary living, the kitchen was upgraded, several closets were added, the attached garage was converted to a family room and a new detached garage was constructed. The experience of living in an Okie house is best conveyed by a quotation from the current owners: "The house has a definite order to it, which promotes a life of simplicity and organization. Each room seems to have its own particular purpose, evoking a sense of intimacy, privacy, and solitude. It is almost like a collection of sanctuaries." —*JDM*

Above: The second floor hallway affords a long vista through a series of doorways articulating a variety of different spaces.

Above top right: This view of the central hallway on the first floor of the Schilling Residence captures a number of details that are characteristic of Mr. Okie's work, including rounded plaster reveals at windows and exterior doors, thin board interior partitions, segmental arched doorways, simple wood wainscoting and wide-board floors.

Above bottom right: The details of the newel post, balusters and handrail of the main stairway reflect woodwork profiles dating from the turn of the nineteenth century.

Facing Page: The first floor library of the Schilling Residence was designed by the architect to be built in natural finish wood including the chimney breast paneling and mantel shelf, vertical board walls, exposed joists, and ceiling boards.

Peter Wentz Farmstead

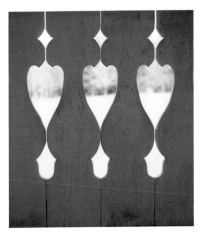

Left: A comprehensive restoration of a country dwelling strongly influenced by Germanic traditions. Careful research revealed characteristic bright colors, balcony, pents, and front entry of settlers from the lower Rhine Valley.

Top: The barn at the Peter Wentz Farmstead was reconstructed and restored to its eighteenth century appearance.

Above: The balcony railing is composed of flat boards cut with matching profiles on their adjacent edges to create decorative positive and negative shapes.

Peter Wentz, Sr., a German from the Palatinate, is listed in the Worcester Township records as early as 1711. An ambitious man, he became a land dealer involved in lumbering, milling, and farming on his considerable acreage in Montgomery County. Evidence concludes that, in 1744, his son Peter Wentz, Jr., knowing that he would inherit 300 acres of his father's 1000-acre property, began to develop his share by building a stone barn on the designated portion. The datestone, found in the remains of a wall, is still legible. This barn was comparatively modest in size, large enough for two or three cows and two horses. The farm's small pigsty was also of stone, a "pig palace." The decision

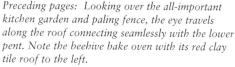

Preceding pages: Looking over the all-important kitchen garden and paling fence, the eye travels along the roof connecting seamlessly with the lower pent. Note the beehive bake oven with its red clay tile roof to the left.

Above: The white plaster walls of the summer kitchen were decorated with black painted spots in a random pattern.

Top: Note the painted plaster wainscot with white spots.

Above: Vista through the rear hall and two-part door to the passage and summer kitchen beyond.

Facing page: The vista across the center hall captures the remarkable original paint color scheme that was documented and recreated as part of the restoration.

to build a shelter for one's domestic animals before one erected a home was in accord with the predisposition of Germans such as Peter Wentz, Sr., who hailed from a rich and fertile valley along the lower Rhine River. In 1758, fourteen years after the barn was completed, Peter Wentz, Jr., designed the handsome and substantial farmhouse pictured here, providing his wife Rosanna and the rest of the family with both comfort and status.

The design of the house followed a mid-century idiom of the mid-Atlantic region, a composite of borrowings from the German tradition and the popular English Georgian developments conspicuous in William Penn's burgeoning colony.

Upon reaching the end of the long lane leading up to the house, one notices the balcony cutting through the cornice of the frontal pent. The rest of the exterior of this five-bay, two-and-half-story, double-pile structure reflects the symmetrical Georgian, measured according to strict rules of proportion. Expressing further basic English Georgian, the six windows in the south end wall and

Above: The blue surrounding the red and white coverlet springs from the German love of bright colors.

Right: The five-plate stove and daybed indicate that this is a room adjoining the kitchen. The stove with folk designs covering each plate, receives its heat through the kitchen wall, a clever innovation.

inner end chimneys carry out the balance and regularity of the period.

The fabric is red shale. Fieldstone and quarries abounded in this region of bountiful natural riches, offering stone that was either lying in the fields or quarried. Peter's choice for the facade of his distinctive house had to be quarried and dressed to the right size. For the rest fieldstone would suffice.

Inside, the insulating palings in the cellar, the five-plate stoves with inscriptions, the house blessing in German, the patterned wainscot, the hardware, the tight, winding stairs, and the "shrouded" summer beam, are all in the Germanic tradition.

During the Revolution the generous size and aspect of Peter's house attracted army personnel delegated to find billeting for the officers. The Wentz house was eminently suitable. General Washington accepted the hospitality of Peter and Rosanna twice, first on October 2, 1777, using it for headquarters just before the Battle of Germantown and some days later, on October 16, when the army was forced to retreat. The General slept in one of the upstairs bedrooms, referred to thereafter as "Washington's room."

In the post-war readjustment period, Peter apparently suffered reverses causing the sale of his house in 1784 to Dewault Bieber and removal to smaller quarters in Whitpain Township, where he and Rosanna lived out their lives. Ten years later the house was bought by Melchior Schultz, and it remained in the family for the next 175 years.

Montgomery County acquired the Farmstead in 1969. The county and dedicated conservationists accepted the responsibility of returning this colorful landmark to the state in which George Washington had seen it in 1777. Management today is under the aegis of the county Department of History and Cultural Arts, supported by the Peter Wentz Farmstead Society, which organizes an educational program. —*MBR*

Muhlenberg House

Peter Muhlenberg Slept Here

The Muhlenberg House is a stunning example of a late-Anglo-German-style dwelling. It is located along the "turnpike" from Philadelphia where the road passes through the small village of Trappe (called Providence during its early years), Montgomery County. The builder was John Jacob Schrack, the Younger, son of the first settler of Trappe. The date of construction has been determined as between 1750 and 1755. Its resemblance to two other extant Germanic-oriented houses of the period, "Grumblethorpe" in Germantown, Philadelphia, and the Peter Wentz House in Worcester Township, confirm the Muhlenberg house as of the same orientation.

Henry Melchior Muhlenberg, having devoted himself to the growth and welfare of the Lutheran Church in Philadelphia from 1761 to 1776 and afterwards in semi-retirement, moved to Trappe in 1776. He bought this substantial house and seven acres to which he made numerous improvements.

The arrival in Trappe of Reverend Henry Muhlenberg and his invalid wife in July 1776 initiated for the house a period of significant recognition. Henry had retired as organizing pastor of the Lutheran Church along the eastern seaboard. He would now fill the role of minister for the Trappe Lutheran Church, a few blocks away from his home, while also providing refuge for citizens fleeing Philadelphia during the war. The Continental Army passed through Trappe with units of the militia enjoying, during the next six months, the hospitality of the Muhlenbergs. General Anthony Wayne and Lord Stirling were given breakfast by Mother Muhlenberg, and, not surprisingly, the soldiers constantly sought help in food, lodging, and medical care.

Henry Muhlenberg had three sons all of whom as youths were sent in 1763 to Halle, Germany, to be educated for

Previous pages: The front facade, which faces the old roadway, was constructed with coursed ashlar sandstone, while the other three facades were constructed with random rubble sandstone.

The deeply curved door hinge (above left) and plate latch (above right) emerge enthusiastically in the German architectural idiom whereas the furniture (top and facing) comes forth more often in plain lines.

the ministry. This next generation distinguished itself in a plethora of remarkable civic responsibilities. The oldest, Peter, born in Trappe, 1746, put his higher education to use in three congregations, in Germantown, Pa., New Jersey, and Virginia. Then, turning from his service to the church to his interest in state affairs, he became a colonel in the Colonial Guard, fought with the Continental Army, became an intimate friend of Washington, and rose to the rank of major general. In 1785 after the war, he became the vice president of Pennsylvania, served in four Congresses, and in 1801 was elected to the Senate. Widely recognized for his abilities, Peter was appointed by President Jefferson as supervisor of Internal Revenue of Pennsylvania. Later, he became collector of the port of Philadelphia. It was in the glow of these achievements and the hospitality of the Muhlenbergs during the war that people were proud to declare "Peter Muhlenberg slept here."

His brother, Frederick Augustus, born 1750, after serving congregations in three Pennsylvania towns, was appointed to the Continental Congress (1777). Later, over a span of years, he was elected to three U.S. Congresses, twice serving as Speaker. Frederick was the first to place his signature on the Bill of Rights and served locally as justice of the peace, judge of Montgomery County, and register of wills. The third brother, G. Henry Ernst Muhlenberg, born 1753, fulfilled for thirty-five years his ministerial destiny at the Trinity Church in Lancaster, assumed the presidency of Franklin College (now Franklin and Marshall), and contributed authoritatively to botanical literature, an area in which he was internationally known as the Linnaeus of America of the eighteenth century.

In 1808, the Muhlenberg family sold the property. Pursuant to this transfer, the ownership did not change hands for four generations, thus establishing the longest period of ownership in one lineage.

Architecturally, the Muhlenberg five-bay, red-sandstone house rises out of an overlapping Anglo-German heritage. From earliest settlement days, German structures were an amalgam. Many people arrived in America from Germany with mental remnants of housing concepts that were in some details medieval, but they turned easily to the new stock items, installing sash windows available in Philadelphia. The pent eaves, deeper than an English pent, the balcony, the long, narrow kitchen, plus two or three more rooms downstairs, the kammer (bedroom), stube (living room), and, in the Muhlenberg house, a parlor are in the German tradition. However, the symmetrical placement of windows, doors and chimneys clearly reflect the English trend expressive of classical Palladian / Georgian "balance" prevalent in English architecture of the period.

In 1990, John Milner, distinguished restoration architect, was called in to plan and specify the restoration process of this rare house. The restoration rested on a critical analysis of the eighteenth-century artifacts found on the property, including the removal of an inappropriate third level added in the nineteenth century. In April 1997, with a grant from the Commonwealth of Pennsylvania and another from the Pew Foundation, plus the financial help of hundreds of citizens in the Perkiomen Valley, the comprehensive restoration was accomplished and the house is well worth a visit. The patriarch Reverend Muhlenberg would be pleased.
—*MBR*

Old Trappe Church

A small backwoods settlement developed near a tavern on the trail of the Perkiomen Creek to the frontier in 1717. As more and more families settled in the clearings in the forest, the community adopted the name Providence (now Trappe). A religious service was few and far between—especially for Lutherans, since the nearest congregation, Falkner Swamp, was twelve miles away.

The Providence Lutherans were left to the doubtful spiritual care of whatever self-styled pastor ventured onto the frontier. Local deacons decided to join nearby Falkner Swamp and Philadephia Lutherans in a call to Europe for a regularly ordained pastor. Henry Melchior Muhlenberg answered the call.

Before the first church was built, Pastor Muhlenberg preached in a barn to the Providence congregation. The congregation was anxious to build a church building and began hauling stones to the site in January 1743. The structure was erected through the spring and summer months and the first service held in the unfurnished interior on September 12, 1743. The building was completed and dedicated on October 6, 1745, at which time the dedication stone was placed over the west portico.

The first church building of Augustus Lutheran Church is still standing and is the oldest unchanged Lutheran Church building in continuous use in the United States. The building predates the Declaration of Independence by one generation and through its simple and sturdy construction speaks to us in the language of another age. It is an expression of the resourcefulness of the pioneers who

Left: This imposing edifice, dedicated in 1745, marked by a massive original style gambrel roof, substantial stone walls, and separate original end wall entrance with arched door opening, has been the site of local Lutheran church meetings since September 1743.

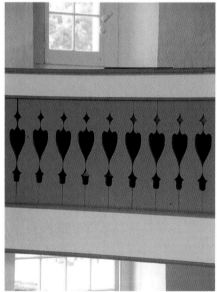

built homes, schools, and churches, and who trained men and women who later helped to carve Liberty out of hard conditions and desperate circumstances.

By 1851 the Old Church was inadequate for the growing congregation and it was resolved to build a new church. The cornerstone was laid on May 18, 1852. The Sanctuary has ten stained-glass windows in the nave depicting twenty-eight scenes from the life and ministry of Jesus. Two other windows depict Martin Luther and Henry Melchior Muhlenberg. These windows were dedicated in June 1987. The Schulmerich electronic carillon plays hymns and strikes the hour for the Trappe community. —HHM

Above left: Much of the church interior retains its original motifs including the magnificent oak carved posts with original stone bases that support the prominent overhead gallery. Original wood pews are at either side of the door entrance.

Top: The original church pews have end doors with distinctive arched tops and magnificent early-German-style wrought iron hinges.

Above: One gallery section has a short outer or facing wall that retains its original vertical boards, cut with German-style hearts that are occasionally seen in mid- to late-eighteenth-century German house staircases in southeast Pennsylvania.

Facing page: From a commanding place, the pastor preached Church doctrine from the original pulpit of English red walnut with overhead sounding board, front and rear paneled wall, and steps.

Saint David's Church

Previous pages: Ecclesiastical architectural motifs and other elements dominate this early Welsh property with 1870s stone vestry to side of the early-eighteenth-century church with steep medieval-like roof with gravestones that encircle both.

Left: Distinctive arched side wall door entry leads into cross aisle with pews at either side.

Facing page: Pews on either side of central alley or aisle lead to altar area at the east end that followed early European traditions. Pulpit at southeast corner has been in use since 1912.

Early eighteenth century churches in original condition are rare in North America. This little stone church, built by a Welsh-speaking Anglican congregation and surrounded on a hill by old hemlocks and gravestones, survives as a monument to a long forgotten age. The church, situated near the border of Newtown and Radnor in Chester County, was "heartily engaged" on September 7, 1714. The cornerstone of the structure was ceremonially laid on May 9, 1715. Parishioners most likely erected the church themselves and completed construction by March 1717. It was dedicated to Saint David, the patron saint of Wales.

The size of the church reflects the needs of a small pioneering community. The roof pitch is noticeably steep. A heavy molded eighteenth-century style cornice is found under the south eaves and simple moldings appear elsewhere around the periphery of the structure. At the north side is a small stone vestry erected in 1871 on the site of a previous vestry. The west end of the church has an enclosed exterior stairway that leads up one flight to the west interior gallery built about 1771. Cornelius Tiebout created a mezzotint engraving of the stairway after a circa 1812 drawing by the well-known architect William Strickland.

The main entrance to the church is through a round arched double door in the middle of the south facade. Originally there was a door in the west end, the outline of which is still visible. There is a single row of large, round-arch windows with shutters around the entire church. No evidence exists that the windows were ever leaded.

The interior of the church, of a single rectangular room, has alleys that divide the area south to north and east to west. At an early date the original open timbered ceiling was replaced by the barrel vaulted ceiling. The flagstone floor was laid in 1925 by the design of the well-known and esteemed local architect R. Brognard Okie. In the first half of the eighteenth century the church had an earthen floor, and titles to actual "pew ground" permitted parishioners to be interred beneath their family's pew. Pew rents were not abolished until 1911.

The present pulpit in the southeast corner of the room, in use since 1912, has a centered altar table to its side that was installed in 1908 by the design of Okie. In keeping with long-held traditions in European churches, the table occupies the east section of the room. The east-facing wooden pews were installed in 1830 that replaced earlier style square pews and a few benches. They were equipped with doors that were removed in 1885 and again replaced prior to 1907 by the present simple paneled wooden doors on all the pews that face the chancel.

The church has received wide recognition as it has been portrayed by a number of American artists including the aforementioned William Strickland (1787–1854) and Andrew Wyeth (1917–present) who created a pen and ink drawing in about 1932. —GDH

Samuel Levis House

Left: Almost monumental in size for its era, the Samuel Levis House from the 1690s reverts to earlier times of high style English architectural expressions. Numerous putlog holes in brick walls for scaffolding during time of construction are still in plain evidence.

Above: Main door with transom on the front facade is topped with a flat brick arch.

Emigrants to the New World often retained their native European manners in what historians refer to as "the transit of civilization." The manorial aspect of the Samuel Levis house in Springfield, Delaware County, is one notable example of how certain affluent Englishmen carried particular traditions of their house building techniques of the sixteenth and seventeenth centuries to America. Levis, born in 1649 in Harby, England, kept alive those customs when, about 1695, he built his house only a few miles west of Philadelphia. His home, on a 150-acre tract he purchased from Owen Foulke in June 1692, vies with the nearby Thomas Massey house in Marple as one of the earliest extant houses in Pennsylvania constructed of brick. The Levis family retained possession of the homestead until 1923.

Following local tradition, the two-story center hall Levis house was built on the edge of a meadow. For such an early house, its large dimensions of 50 feet by 24 feet were more than adequate to provide for his wife, Elizabeth Claytor, and their seven children. Perhaps some of his slaves took residence in the house. Intricately patterned Flemish brick bond appears on all exterior walls. The dark brick headers lend the house its local sobriquet—the "Checkerboard House." As poignant reminders of early construction tech-

Above: Early style six-panel door leads into the parlor that appears at the west side of the first floor center hall. Seventeenth century primitive English style press cupboard and gateleg table complement early architectural elements of room.

Facing page: Door opening in center hall flanked by very early style settle leads into parlor with view of side of gateleg table and end wall fireplace with original mantle shelf at top and paneled door to side.

Above: Bedroom on second floor above the first floor dining room has typically small end wall fireplace and window at its side. Very early type casement window appears above bed.

Right: In the original house plan, the kitchen area, with a walk-in fireplace, was located in the basement. The brick floor withstood heavy foot traffic for numerous generations.

niques, there are, curiously, strategically placed gaps that remain in the brickwork as putlog holes for scaffolding poles that were utilized during the erection of the brick walls.

As a departure from the often seen English-based hall and parlor arrangement, there were originally two rooms at each side of the nine-foot wide centered hall. At one side of the hall at the front was the dining room with exposed summer beam, original fireplace opening, and early style fireplace surround. A rare original casement window frame is retained on the front wall. A magnificent partition wall with 16-inch-wide boards separates this room from the rear room, which may have been the office of Samuel Levis. Superb original oak flooring remains. At the opposite side of the hall at the front is the parlor that basically maintains the same features as the dining room. To the rear was originally one room that apparently joined the hall in ell-formation.

A Baroque-looking staircase with heavy newel posts accented with original finials and pendants all within the confines of the "office room" ascends to the second floor and into the attic. Five uneven-sized second floor rooms come off an ell-shaped hall. All the rooms but one retain their original oak flooring. Two rooms each have an exposed ceiling beam in addition to the large full house width master bedroom that has an almost centered fireplace on an exquisitely paneled end wall.

The embanked nature of the house afforded the inclusion of a kitchen in the basement. An off-center cooking fireplace with a massive iron crane has small closets at either side. Two original doors lead to double mirror images and prominent brick-lined arched vaults that served as probable root cellars. —*GDH*

Above: Distinct attention to detail is seen in the decorative belt course that Thomas Massey incorporated into the east gable end wall.

Right: Various telescoping sections of the Thomas Massey house complex are all composed of different local materials. At the extreme right is the earliest existing section and it peculiarly has no entrance door.

Thomas Massey House

The house that stands in the Broomall section of Marple Township on Lawrence Road in Delaware County has a section that may be one of the oldest brick structures in Pennsylvania. Built by Thomas Massey in 1696, it stood adjacent to an even earlier building that was apparently constructed of frame or logs. About 1730, a two-story stone section replaced the earlier structure and a stone wing may have been added at that time. Then, at about the time of the Civil War, the kitchen wing was expanded to two stories.

Today the house stands on a single acre—all that is left of the original 300-acre plantation. An existing indenture indicates that Thomas Massey, likely born in the 1660s in Cheshire, England, bought the land in September 1696 as part of a much larger 500-acre tract that was originally granted by patent in January 1683. The land remained in the family until 1925. In 1963 the Massey house was purchased by a Massey descendant and then given to Marple Township for restoration.

Above: A single room composes the first floor of the stone middle house section with substantially sized fireplace and original cupboard on its side.

Facing page: A single room, with walk-in fireplace at the rear corner and casement window frame on the back wall, occupies the entire first floor of the earliest section built in 1690s.

The two-story brick eastern section has decorative Flemish bond brick patterning on both the front facade and east end wall and less showy English bond on the rear wall. Curiously, there is no front door to this section indicating that the main entrance was in the adjacent earlier structure. The one first floor room has a walk-in style fireplace in the rear corner. Much of the casement window frame on the front wall has miraculously survived. In addition, original walnut casement window frames adorn both front and rear walls of the one second-floor room. Ceiling timbers are seen in both of these rooms. The basement under this section contains two massive arched stone vaults.

The two-story stone middle section retains its original 270-year-old six-paneled front door and door frame. A large jambed fireplace with a flanking cupboard with original doors and butterfly shelves is seen at the west end wall of the one first floor room. The stairway in the rear corner

has original oak wood. The second floor room's west wall has a small fireplace with an arched opening with its original unpainted poplar paneling.

The west stone section of the house that contains the kitchen may have been built as early as 1730 and was expanded to two full stories about 1860. The first story of one room has a walk-in fireplace on its west end wall and a stairway on the opposite wall that leads to a second floor room where no fireplace was ever included.

A major restoration project in the late 1960s brought back many original-like features and motifs. The Massey house provides a microcosm of many cultural and material adaptations that farmers in the rural Pennsylvanian countryside experienced during the late seventeenth century through the middle third of the nineteenth century. Each house section reflects different conditions and constraints the owners experienced at the time of construction. —GDH

Datestone of 1769 inscribed "R + D" for Richard Dutton, a local affluent farmer, appears at end wall under the peak. The datestone is incorporated within a stone arch.

Chichester Meeting House

Many Europeans suffered persecution at the hands of innumerable despots and tyrants in the seventeenth and eighteenth centuries. As an ecclesiastical leader of those tumultuous times of religious unrest, George Fox founded the Quaker movement in 1652. When he gathered with people of like persuasion, he had to settle for houses, barns, or whatever other structure might be suitable as places for the glorification of God. Prior to the 1690s, Quakers rarely erected specific buildings as places of worship. But when Quakers or Friends as they were known, first began migrating to southwest New Jersey in the 1670s and southeast Pennsylvania in the 1680s, they enjoyed a freedom to meet openly as was guaranteed by that earliest of great American Quakers—William Penn. As part of this new allowance for spiritual-minded expression, Quakers were licensed to construct buildings of whatever form or style that fit their needs.

Although built as late as 1769, Chichester Meeting House, which stands in Upper Chichester Township in Delaware County, ranks as one of the earliest existing meeting houses in all of Pennsylvania in near pristine condition. It is reflective of an earlier period. The incorporated plan survives as one of the best remaining demonstrations of a blending of English meeting patterns and meeting house plans. The rather compact structure replaced the

Previous pages: End wall of meeting house has centered door with flanking early type twelve-over-twelve windows. Other early meeting houses in southeast Pennsylvania similarly have end wall entrances.

Left: Rows of early style pews flank the ten-plate stove in the east room.

Facing page: The smaller of the two rooms, the west room includes a fireplace in the southwest corner and a single fixed bench along both the west wall and the north wall (out of view).

original 24-foot square stone 1680s meeting house that was destroyed by fire in January 1769. A semi-circular tablet adorns the center of the gable just under the peak and bears the inscription *R + D 1769*. The initials are thought to represent a local affluent farmer—Richard Dutton, Chichester's most active member.

Chichester Meeting House stands one-story high. Pairs of evenly spaced windows punctuate all four walls and on three of the walls a central door divides the windows. Distinctive trapezoidal stone lintels accent the top of all exterior wall openings. On the interior, a transverse wooden partition wall divides the building into two meeting rooms of unequal size. The smaller west room features a fireplace in the southwest corner and a single fixed bench along the north and west walls. The larger east room includes both a similar bench affixed to the partition and two rows of fixed facing benches on a tiered platform along the east wall.

Most extant American meeting house designs of the period place the main entrance and elevated seating area, known as the facing bench, on the long walls. At Chichester, both features are located in the gable or end walls. The designers partitioned the building in a manner in which the facing bench was only included in one of the meeting rooms.

In the middle of the east room stands an old ten-plate cast iron stove. Both rooms communicate by means of a central and southern doorway in the paneled and vertical boarded partition. A central aisle leads from the front door to the facing benches that separate rows of movable benches on either side of the partition.

Out of the perplexing array of specific styles of Quaker meeting houses throughout approximately 300 years of various building traditions, Chichester Meeting House retains an almost unique position. Both the fabric and structure of the building as dictated by complex cultural influences stands as a certifiable bridge between the times when English Quakers had virtually no physical place to call their own and the more advanced American houses of worship in the late eighteenth century and beyond. —*GDH*

Spring House at Poole Farm

In the mid-Atlantic area the term *spring house* often refers literally to "a house built over a spring," the primary purpose being to provide a cool environment in which to store dairy and other perishable food items. In exploiting the cooling effects of underground water, an early type of refrigeration was created.

The spring house shown here is located adjacent to a spring, the water entering through a small opening in the side wall of the lower section where it then pooled into a trough, exiting the building through a similar opening in the opposite side. At one time the water might have then been piped into a cistern as a source of potable water— streams were not acceptable sources for human consumption, since they were all too likely contaminated by livestock.

Entrance to the lower section of the spring house was through a doorway located at the bottom of a short stairway. Inside, a walkway went almost the full way into the house, surrounded on three sides by the running water. In this rested numerous crocks, jugs, and canisters. The effect of the cool spring water kept the contents of the crocks at a temperature usually close to fifty-five-degrees Fahrenheit. The entire room maintained a fairly cool environment, so quite often additional items were stored on shelving. The ceiling was plastered between the exposed joists to prevent moisture from entering the main section above.

The main section in this spring house includes a small fireplace, an indication of its use as a living space. This particular spring house has three windows, not the usual two. The doorway is in the northern wall, roughly five feet above ground level, so a stairway would have been an exterior element. A bedroom loft was accessed via a step ladder-like stairway. —GG

Garrett-Booth-Cheyney Farm

Preceding pages: English farmers had two-level bank barns—called English Lake District barns—constructed at their homesteads in the counties surrounding Philadelphia starting likely in the middle third of the eighteenth century. The Booth stone barn was built about 1790. Note: exterior of main house appears on pages 2–3.

Facing page: The main house complex has a twentieth-century porch addition that appears to the side of the stone walled kitchen built in the same general era.

Above left: The 1810 house section has end to end rooms on the first floor in Penn plan-like arrangement. The front room has a corner fireplace with a Federal-style surround and overhead ceiling joists are exposed.

Above right: A single bedroom occupies the second floor of the circa 1790 section with exposed joists and a small end wall fireplace with original surround.

Ancient Bethel Road in what would become Delaware County was originally laid out in 1686. Among a number of other local families with properties, a contemporary road survey mentions the land of Thomas Garrett. Garrett, born in 1652 in England, came to Pennsylvania before 1682. Thomas apparently constructed a log house and the land later exchanged hands a few times. Robert Booth bought the log house and 100 acres in 1712 and the farm remained in the family until the 1830s. After a few other owners, the Cheyney family bought the land and farmed it for more than a hundred years. There are presently three main structures on the homestead grounds—the main two-section house complex, an extensively reconstructed barn, and a relocated log house.

The smaller of the two house sections of the main house is a two-story one-room-deep stone structure whose wood-work and trim indicate a 1790 construction date (some evidence in contention suggests a far earlier date of 1721). The house was apparently located immediately adjacent to the log house. Around 1810 a large two-story two-room-deep stone addition replaced the dismantled log structure.

The small 1790 section is of two-bay construction. Each floor consists of one room. On the first floor, a large walk-in cooking fireplace at the front corner away from the main door probably complemented the fireplace in the log structure. Original windows, front door, exterior shutters, and window and door trim all reflect the late-eighteenth-century construction date. The second floor has a small hall and a single bedroom with diminutive fireplace and exposed joists.

The larger section of 1810 also features two-bay construction. The first floor is two rooms deep, each room

Above: The single bedroom on the second floor of the circa 1790 house section has a staircase with a distinctive spiral effect or winder stair that leads to the attic via an original door.

Right: In the first floor kitchen of the circa 1790 section is a corner cooking fireplace with non-original lintel and exposed beaded ceiling joists.

with a corner fireplace on the end wall that stand back-to-back, and ceiling joists and floor boards above are original. The second floor has two small bedrooms toward the front and one large bedroom and an adjacent hall at the rear.

The small barn, only 39 feet by 33 feet, is a two story banked structure patterned after barns found in the Northwest Lake District in England. The top floor was used for threshing and crop storage and the basement for stabled farm stock. Exterior walls are all stone and three distinctive arched animal door openings appear on the front wall. As virtually the entire interior has been gutted, the age of the barn is fundamentally indeterminate.

The Southey log house was removed from its previous site one-and-one-half miles from the Sarum farm in 1972. Many of the original logs from the log walls were saved but several had to be replaced. The small log structure, 18 feet by 24 feet, is of two-story construction (see photos on pp. 6–11). Diamond notching, which appears at the corners, is very unusual for a southeast Pennsylvania log structure. Each floor level has back to back rooms in Penn Plan form with corner fireplaces and exposed ceiling joists. The reconstructed rear room fireplace on the second floor is conjectural. —GDH

in Grist Mill

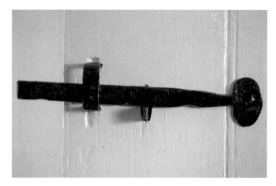

Left: The miller's two-story house, constructed from local stone, is a three-bay structure with chimneys at each end wall.

Early style wrought door latch, held in place by wrought nail in disk at one end and metal staple toward opposite end, adds a touch of authentic antiquity to second floor bedroom.

Sharing a common trait with churches from the same era, very early eighteenth-century grist mills in the Greater Delaware Valley are rare. They should be. The basic inner structure of these highly utilitarian buildings wore out after literally rattling around for more than half a century. That truth, along with the fact that their basic economic vitality was lost in post-pioneering communities, spelled the usual demise of these rural icons. One rare survivor from 1704, built by Nathaniel and Mary Newlin, is found along the West Branch of Chester Creek in Concord Township. It was actually preceded by two other water-powered mills constructed by Nicholas Newlin, a Quaker and father of Nathaniel. The Newlin family had arrived in the New World from Ireland in 1683. In that same year, William Penn granted a five-hundred-acre tract of land to the family and all three mills were later erected.

Grain was ground at the mill continuously from its construction until 1941. Realizing its extreme historic value as an interpretative site, E. Mortimer Newlin established the Nicholas Newlin Foundation in 1957 thus assuring preservation of the mill, other buildings, and 150 surrounding acres. By 1962, restoration of the mill was achieved and the site then opened as a museum. It was not until 1992, when the trustees of the foundation decided to reconstruct the mill, that the old inner structure was dismantled so that it could be rebuilt and more knowledge of the original building could be obtained.

Early style stone construction is seen on all exterior walls that are decidedly graduated in thickness from the ground up. Three floors with typical inner mill machinery denote the probable interior layout of the mill. The top, or bin floor, features a bolter, where ground meal was sifted and separated into lots by texture, and where a grain bin was fed from loaded wagons through end wall doors on this level. On the middle, or grain floor, a hopper received grain by gravity from above that fed into a damsel or square shaft

175

Above: Side-by-side doors at rear wall of the northwest room on second floor are for access to first floor and attic. The doors were so positioned to conserve space in the establishment of the original house plan.

Right: Most interior elements of rural vernacular architecture appear on the first floor of the miller's house including winder stair, end wall fireplace with mantle shelf and wood flooring.

that emptied grain into the eye of the upper of two mill-stones. It was between the top runner stone and the stationary lower bedstone where grain was actually ground. Subsequently, grain appeared as meal around the periphery of the stones where it was then discharged into a meal trough on the lowest level, or meal floor.

Water to power the mill was led from a millpond to the water wheel by a flume or channel. The amount of water to the wheel was controlled by the flume gate, which, when raised, allowed pressurized emergent water to strike the buckets of the water wheel that caused it to revolve. The spokes of the wheel were connected to a main shaft that transmitted power by a series of gears and other engaged elements and ultimately to the runner stone that allowed grain to be ground.

The fully restored structure, thought to be the only original fully functioning colonial grist mill in the nation, is accompanied on the site by the Miller's house, perhaps built by a Newlin descendant, and the Trimble house, constructed by a local sawmill operator. —GDH

Top: The full mill structure, consisting of three sections, was constructed in three distinctly different eras—1704, 1739, and about 1850. The earliest section appears at the lower right near the steps to the road.

Above: The overshot waterwheel appears on the ground floor of the 1739 stone mill section that is adjacent to the 1704 stone section.

Facing page: Stone wall and exposed ceiling joists are seen on the second floor of the 1704 section of the mill. The gear mechanism was relocated from another area of this section.

John Chad House

Above: The Chad house was built into a bank that afforded a kitchen area in the basement. The large cooking fireplace with rear wall bake oven appears to the side of the exterior door that in turn is adjacent to staircase to first floor.

Facing page: Although quite small in size, circa 1725 John Chad House includes prominent eighteenth-century embellishments such as distinctive end wall pent eaves and pent roofs on three walls.

Nestled in an embankment in the gently rolling terrain of southern Chester County is the early 1720s John Chad house, one of the most enchanting vernacular homes in the Greater Brandywine Valley. Innumerable motorists, visitors, and historians alike have admired the house for many years. John Chad hired John Wyeth, a local stonemason, to construct his house, which was probably completed by about 1725. He is credited as the founder of Chadds Ford, as he established several businesses that included a ferry service and a tavern.

This venerable stone-walled but diminutive two-story structure was built into a slope of land, making this a genuine bank house. Short projecting pent roofs at the top of the first floor level appear on three walls. In addition, short-pent eaves, which occur on many pre-1800 houses in southeast Pennsylvania, appear at the top of the second story at every wall. A prominent beehive-oven extends from the basement kitchen on the end wall nearest the road.

Setting the tone of the extreme antiquity of the interior is the original front door and door frame. Visitors pass through and into the Great Hall on the first floor, which is open toward the east side but has several features at its west end wall with a fireplace in the corner, a closet in the middle, and stairs to both the second floor and basement. Most of the wall panels are original, including the distinctive

Above: Early windows with original frames flank the arched corner fireplace at the front of the house in the east room or parlor on the first floor. The wood surround of both the fireplace plus the open sectioned wall unit above is original.

Facing page: The second floor east bedroom, with corner fireplace and original floorboards, is divided from the rest of the floor by a magnificent original partition wall of vertical feather edged boards. At the corner fireplace all of the wood of the chimney breast is original.

chimney breast paneling. The fine detailing of the woodwork bespeaks the status of Chad in his community. The ceiling height is just over seven-and-one-half feet, about average for a house built in the early eighteenth century. To the east of the great room is the parlor with a fireplace at the front corner of the end wall. The usable space in this room was only slightly less than that in the great room. The partition wall that separates the two rooms consists of original one-inch-thick feather-edged yellow poplar boards.

The original spiral stairway led to the second floor, and there is an in-place stairway window. The small upper hallway leads into two chambers. The first is the bedchamber, whose west wall surface has a projection that incorporates two large chimney flues from fireplaces from below. The second room is the master bedchamber, which features the most visually appealing fireplace in the house. Its woodwork is almost completely original.

The basement, consisting of two rooms, contains the large kitchen that is the most extensively restored room in the entire house. The kitchen opens to grade at the west-end of the house. The most notable trait is the large walk-in fireplace with an unusual double beam of oak that assists in supporting the masonry wall above. At the back corner was an opening for a beehive oven. Adjacent to the kitchen was a root cellar or keeping room to store root vegetables. —GDH

William Brinton House

Separated by distinctly different times of erection and modes of construction, the two sections of the William Brinton House stand in unqualified contrast to each other. The earlier and medieval-like larger section is of two full stories and of native stone, while the other one and one-half story section is quite small and of nineteenth-century frame construction. It is the larger section that demands special consideration.

It is thought that William Brinton constructed the earlier house section in 1704 that still bears his name. Brinton, who came to America in the spring of 1684 with his father William and mother Ann, was born in Worcestershire, England, in August 1670. The family had first come to New Castle County, Delaware, and then settled at a site just north of the Brinton House where they built a crude cabin of poplar planks.

The early house section has each end wall that is distinguished with an interior positioned brick chimney and a typical eighteenth-century pent eave at the top of the second floor. The roof pitch is steep, as if so often found on early houses. A short projecting pent roof appears across the entire front façade. Through the painstaking research of G. Edwin Brumbaugh, the noted restoration architect, original-style leaded glass windows were reproduced on all four exterior walls.

In typical English style, the first floor is of a hall and parlor arrangement. The front door opened into the hall that functioned as a general use area, as was noted in a 1751 inventory. The fireplace at the paneled end wall has a surprisingly small opening. A transverse partition wall, constructed of non-original replacement boards, separates the hall from the parlor. The parlor served the family as a pri-

Right: The medieval-like manner of construction is unmistakable in the very early eighteenth- century house of William Brinton. Its distinctive end wall pent eaves and front wall pent roof typify numerous eighteenth-century houses in southeast Pennsylvania.

Above: Family activities, often reserved for the first floor in many pre-1750 rural homes, took place in the cavernous basement kitchen. The massive walk-in fireplace, where cooking was done, included a rare fully interior bake oven.

Right: The front facade door opens into the large hall of the first floor. With paneled fireplace wall and reproduction casement windows on front and rear walls, the room's early appearance is faithfully completed with period furnishings.

vate area with a fireplace at the end wall with a closet at each side. As found in the hall, there is, oddly, only one exposed ceiling beam. The family used the parlor as sleeping quarters and for other general purposes.

The second floor is broken up into five rooms. Separate hallway sections lead into the first and second rooms that together were originally one large room. At the west end is a large bedroom with a small end wall fireplace with a raised hearth.

Much family activity in the Brinton House occurred in the three-room basement. The main basement room functioned both as a kitchen for eating at a large stretcher table and for cooking that was performed in a cavernous end wall fireplace. A large beehive oven is situated at the left of the fireplace and is unusual as it was built entirely within the confines of the house walls instead of protruding from the exterior wall. A stairway to the first floor is located to the left of the oven. Double door openings on a transverse wall lead into two storage rooms where objects such as spinning wheels, a churn, cheese press and barrels for root crops were kept. —GDH

Gilpin House

The Gilpin House at Brandywine Battlefield Park, just east of Chadds Ford, is unique in the entire Greater Brandywine Valley. The proportions and disposition of all three sections are distinctly different and, along with the various family occupations, offer both a long and intricate history. A one-hundred-acre tract was originally held in trust for Hannah Glover, the daughter of Alice Glover who later married John Brunsden. The Brunsdens settled in this area about 1684. Later, Hannah married Joseph Gilpin in 1691. The Gilpins transferred land in 1729 to their son Joseph Jr. who may have been responsible for the construction of the 1745 two-story stone main front section of the Gilpin house.

Gideon Gilpin, born circa 1737 and third son of Joseph Jr., built the rear stone one-story unit with loft in 1782. It is the frame one-and-a-half-story kitchen wing that is to the side of the two-story main section whose construction date is the most in doubt. The Direct Tax of 1798 lists a frame kitchen but the cited dimensions do not match the size of the present kitchen. Later, in an advertisement, the stone and frame dwelling "with kitchen attached thereto" was put to public sale in 1827. In 1848, Benson Lossing

Above: The rear first floor room of the 1745 stone section features a walk-in fireplace in the corner and single window on the rear wall. As all other rooms in all house sections exposed joists are in full view.

Right: The Revolutionary War-era stone addition at the rear of the house has a genuinely massive walk-in cooking fireplace. More exposed ceiling joists are seen along with numerous objects related to food preparation.

sketched the first graphic recording of the house that illustrates all house sections including the kitchen wing fronted by a narrow porch. A few observers contend the frame section dates from the early eighteenth century, and was subsequently moved adjacent to the main block.

The main house unit is a rare surviving rural example of the Tradesman House or Penn Plan House style. Penn houses were common in urban Philadelphia where street frontage was at a premium and therefore dictated the narrow fronts of houses that are still seen today. The main house reflects these narrow dimensions, as the facade has only a single door and a single window to its side. The first floor is two pile (two rooms deep) with a front and a rear room, each with a corner fireplace placed back-to-back. Overhead beams are in full view, although few are original. The second floor originally duplicated the first floor arrangement except for the rear room that presently has no fireplace.

The rear house section, almost square, is composed of a single large room with a walk-in fireplace and a loft above. The frame wing section at the front, in accord with early building practices, has a steeply pitched roof. The exterior, covered with horizontal weatherboarding, has a south facing front facade with a single window at each side of a centered door. A chimney appears at the east end wall. On the interior is a single first floor room with exposed overhead beaded beams and reproduction casement windows, with leaded diamond-shaped panes on the front wall. Stairways to the basement and loft above are located at the east end wall next to the large walk-in fireplace. —GDH

The Gilpin House at Brandywine Battlefield Park is administered by the Pennsylvania Historical and Museum Commission.

Barns-Brinton House

One of Pennsylvania's most notable early-eighteenth-century vernacular houses, the Barns-Brinton House is difficult to miss, literally—it sits only a few feet south from the shoulder of Route One in Chester County. The house stands, however, just north of the original road, known in the eighteenth century as "ye Great road to Nottingham," an important roadway laid out between Chester and Baltimore in 1707.

The house, thought to have been built in 1714, was likely originally constructed as a public tavern with bar, overnight accommodations, and private home. The two first-floor rooms were divided into what may have been a public tavern and private area. Two bedrooms on the second floor were similarly split between public and private space with no doorway between the two rooms. The full cellar provided storage space.

William Barns, a blacksmith, bought 104 acres at the west side of the Brandywine about 1710. On November 27, 1722, William sought to operate a tavern by obtaining a license, but the actual license was not issued until 1726. In 1753, James Brinton bought the tavern and property for private use. The homestead remained in the family until the 1850s.

Despite its small dimensions, the early Brinton house still looms as an imposing edifice. Its diminutive end wall renders a distinct appearance of verticality to the house. Brick on all four walls, the front wall was adorned with ornate Flemish bond brickwork while the remaining walls were of English bond. Distinctive early style pent roofs above the first story and recreated casement windows appear around most of the exterior of the house.

The floor plan is of a hall and parlor arrangement. The original oak front door opens into the hall or the tavern room where travelers enjoyed food and drink. A large nine-foot-wide walk-in style cooking fireplace warmed early travelers, but the fireplace lacked the usually included bake oven. The original inglenook seat adjacent to the window

The small but powerfully expressed architectural elements bespeak the prominent status of William Barns in the second decade of the eighteenth century when his home was erected. Careful and refined brick workmanship is seen on all four walls.

Left: The first floor parlor has one of the most astonishing early-eighteenth-century house fireplace walls in all of Pennsylvania. A fully developed bolection molding, mantle shelf, chimney breast paneling, five panel door, stairway, and oak flooring are all miraculously original.

Above: Detail of fireplace wall in second floor bedroom shows sections of ventilating screen and fireplace mantle shelf.

Following pages: The first floor hall first served as a tavern room in the 1720s. Similar to that found in the parlor, all original architectural details of the fireplace wall, save the mantle shelf, have endured. The most spectacular survival is the inglenook seat at the rear wall.

has amazingly survived. The non-original cage type bar, recreated from surviving evidence, accents the entire room. The parlor has a 6-foot-wide fireplace at the end wall with a magnificent bolection molding. As seen in the hall, the fireplace wall is paneled.

Both second floor rooms have paneled end walls with centered fireplaces. Likely as a way to maintain desired exterior proportions, the ceiling height is about one foot shorter than that found in the rooms on the first floor. The west bedroom has a bolection molding around the fireplace. Wood ventilating screens above the closet doors on the fireplace walls in both bedrooms are partially original.

The house stands as a tangible passageway to and reminder of another age that has long since disappeared. Fortunately, this gem of very early house architecture in southeast Pennsylvania has been preserved through the efforts of the Chadds Ford Historical Society. Extensive restoration began on the house in the 1970s. —GDH

Keepsake

Preceding pages: The original two-story house, dating from the late 1820s, was thoroughly restored and a new one-story wing was built to the east in 2002. Both sections have dark granite exterior walls, brick chimneys, and slate roofs.

Above left: The parlor on the first floor consists of two spaces, each with a fireplace, joined by a wide doorway passage. The woodwork details are consistent with the Federal style of the early nineteenth century.

Above right: This small reception room and library is located at the front of the original house, across the central hall from the front parlor. The plaster walls, ceilings and random-width oak flooring throughout the house are original.

Facing page: The smokehouse, added in the mid-nineteenth century, was in poor condition and was reconstructed to serve as a den. The corner fireplace and antique paneled mantelpiece were introduced, along with the antique brick floor. The ceiling joists were salvaged from the original smokehouse.

Built in the late 1820s on the north bank of the Brandywine River in Chadds Ford, the house known as "Keepsake" is a two-and-one-half-story gable-roof structure representing a vernacular interpretation of the Federal style. The exterior walls are constructed of an indigenous blue-black colored stone known as Brandywine Blue Granite. The front facade faces south and the stone is laid in a coursed ashlar pattern, while the stone on the other facades is laid in a random or "rubble" pattern. A one-story stone kitchen wing, original to the house, projects from the west end of the rear facade. The main house and kitchen wing have red brick cornices and slate roofs. A low

two-story stone addition, covered with stucco and thought to have been a smokehouse, was built during the mid-nineteenth century adjacent to the east end of the rear facade.

The interior of the main house is organized around a central hall with a stairway, flanked on the first floor by two rooms on each side, each having a fireplace. Two rooms also flanked the hall on each side at the second floor, but were heated by stoves in lieu of fireplaces. Although a small amount of the original interior woodwork was removed during alterations in the twentieth century, the basic original floor plan, plaster walls and ceilings, doors, windows, several fireplace mantels and wood flooring survived intact.

Above: Adjacent to the reception room is the dining room with its original fireplace and woodwork. The restored house and new addition, designed by architect John Milner, complement the owners' collection of American furniture and decorative arts.

Facing page: The arched doorway in the new gallery, connecting the original house and addition, frames a view of the gardens designed by landscape architect Jonathan Alderson.

The details of the woodwork reflect the transition from colonial to Greek revival styles, and are typical of the 1820s and 1830s in the Delaware Valley.

Keepsake was acquired in 1999 by new owners, who were intent on restoring the house, building a new addition, and creating several complementary new outbuildings. An easement donated by previous owners to the Brandywine Conservancy required that any new addition be placed on the east side of the original house to minimize its visibility from the passing roadway. Such a restriction did not represent a hardship, since the east facade was largely devoid of architectural detail, and may even have been anticipated by the original builders as the logical location for later expansion. Working with John Milner Architects, the owners planned and built a one-story addition to provide expanded living space on the first floor. The addition is linked to the main house by a low "hyphen" structure incorporating a hallway and porch. The exterior walls of the addition were constructed with the blue-black granite laid in a rubble pattern, and the roof was covered with slate. The main house was carefully restored and improved. A new garden house and carriage house were designed and constructed with materials and details similar to those of the house. —JDM

Abiah Taylor House and Farm

Above: The Taylor house and barn that stand across from each other on a country lane are so positioned so as to take maximum advantage of the terrain they each occupy.

Left: The restored interior of the Samuel Taylor Lancashire-style ground barn echoes its original functions of crop storage and farm stock stabling. Through the threshing doors of the south wall the 1724 Taylor brick house looms in the background.

Only under rare circumstances do both a very early house and early barn survive at the same farmstead in Pennsylvania or anywhere else in North America. The Abiah Taylor homestead house, just west of West Chester, has an original datestone that reads *1724 A T D*. It was determined that the ground barn across the ancient farm road was constructed in 1753. Each of these structures has an absorbing history.

The Abiah Taylor family first arrived in Chester County in 1702, from Didcote in Berkshire, England, northwest of London. At that time, Taylor constructed his first house, of either log or frame construction, which was replaced a decade later with a small stone structure. In another decade, he built the present three-bay two- story house as an addition to the stone building. Ornate Flemish brick bond appears on the south and west walls while simpler English bond appears on the north and east walls. A single T-shaped chimney is seen at the north end wall. Each end wall has the typical eighteenth-century projecting pent eave at the top of the second floor. Carefully reconstructed casement windows adorn each wall of the house. Early style and distinctive brick segmental-like arches appear above the first floor windows on the front facade. The first floor, consisting of two rooms, has an original cooking fireplace on the north wall. The second floor, however, has one large room at the north end and two smaller rooms appear at the south side. Despite a number of alterations, the house retains much of its original appearance because of an extensive restoration

Above: South end wall has distinctive eigh-teenth-century architectural features with pent eaves and a pent roof interrupted by a balcony and leaded glass casement windows. New wood addition abuts the south end wall.

Right: The new addition, designed by John Milner, incorporates an early-eighteenth-century Pennsylvania staircase acquired from the estate of prominent architect G. Edwin Brumbaugh.

in 1995. The Taylor home sits on a naturally occurring hillock that was obviously pre-selected as the most appropriate site for the house. The early barn across the road stands in prominent view.

The 1753 stone ground barn that replaced the original pioneer barn some thirty years after the house was built was erected when Samuel Taylor owned the homestead. It has a peculiar style of construction that is referred to as Lancashire. These rare American barns are patterned after similar structures in the Lancashire area of northwest England. The Taylor barn, which retains much of its original basic fabric, barely survived a devastating tornado in the 1970s. Both the original early style roof along with the east stone wall, rebuilt in the late 1990s, had collapsed. The barn, of typical early style three bay construction, is 50 feet at the side wall and 28 feet at the end wall. The threshing floor occupies the middle bay and uneven width stabling bays are at either side. Above each stable and threshing floor, farm crops were stored after harvesting. All walls are pierced with vertical splayed loopholes or *balistratus* for interior ventilation. The south side wall retains segmental arches over the two windows, an uncommon trait for any stone barn of any era. The barn presently stands in a singularly important position as the earliest positively identified barn that retains its basic original form and fabric in the entire state of Pennsylvania. —GDH

Above: This corner fireplace in the new addition has an antique wood mantel shelf and a raised limestone hearth. The curved feature at the ceiling above the mantel is a partial masonry arch that supports the second floor fireplace. Included are overhead exposed joists.

Right: The dining room of the early brick house has a six-foot-wide fireplace with candle niches in the rear wall. Missing elements of the original woodwork were restored based on surviving physical evidence. A bronze sculpture Carolyn with Cattle Egrets *rests on an early-eighteenth-century English gateleg table.*

The William Peters House

Preceding pages: The 1750 William Peters House was dismantled, moved, and reconstructed with precision and accuracy by the owners and their architect Albert Kruse. The hand-molded brick walls are laid in the Flemish bond pattern on the principal facades, and in the English and common bond patterns on the secondary facades.

Left: The dining room, located to the east of the front hall and adjacent to the kitchen, has been reconstructed to its exact original size with its original woodwork including window trim, chair rail, baseboard, and fireplace wall paneling.

Facing page: The center hall is divided at its mid-point by a wood framed arched opening that establishes a hierarchy between the front and rear of the house. The parlor and dining room, flanking the front hall, were intended for the reception and entertainment of guests. The kitchen was accessible from the rear hall.

Following pages: The original wood paneling and door and window trim in all of the rooms, including the original front parlor, were documented with drawings and photographs prior to their careful removal and installation in the reconstructed house. The paint colors were selected by the owners, based on historical precedent and compatibility with their American furniture and decorative arts collections.

The story of the William Peters House is as much about a splendid vernacular Georgian masterpiece of the mid-eighteenth century, as it is about the remarkable effort that rescued it from certain destruction and gave it new life as a residence two centuries later. William Peters, an English Quaker, earned prosperity as a maker of cloth and an operator of industrial enterprises along the Chester Creek in Aston Township, Chester County. In 1750, he and his wife Eleanor erected a fine brick house, near their mills, that spoke of their prominent station in the community. Aston and other townships were later incorporated in the newly created Delaware County.

The two-and-one-half-story building, with formal facades and a symmetrical floor plan organized around a center hall, represented a level of sophistication that was unusual in the early rural settlements of southeastern Pennsylvania. Primitive Hall, built in 1738 and documented on the following pages, is another example. The exterior walls were constructed of handmade brick, laid in a Flemish bond pattern on the south and west facades, and a combination of English and common bonds on the north and east facades. Flemish bond was often reserved for facades that the owner regarded as the most prominent and visible when passing by or approaching the building. The front door, with a second floor door and balcony above, was placed at the center of the south facade. The doors were flanked with two nine-light over nine-light windows on each side. A pent roof extended across all four facades

between the first- and second-floor windows. On the first and second floors, two rooms were positioned on each side of the center hall containing the principal staircase. Each room had a fireplace located on the interior wall dividing the front rooms from the rear rooms, and was embellished with fine woodwork, more formal in the front rooms and less formal in the rear. The kitchen occupied the space to the right of the center hall at the rear, and contained a small winding staircase to the servants' quarters above.

When the current owners discovered the house in 1964, it was in deplorable condition, having been partially damaged by fire and without a roof for two years. The Township Fire Marshall had declared the building a hazard and was in the process of ordering its demolition. Recognizing that the tragic loss of a very important and largely intact early building was imminent, and that restoration at its existing location was not an option, arrangements were quickly made for its purchase and relocation to a new site. Working with architect Albert Kruse, the owners secured the building and thoroughly documented its original exterior and interior features with measured drawings and photographs. The woodwork was carefully removed and catalogued. The brick walls were then dismantled and all of the materials moved to the new site approximately six miles away in Chester County. With abundant skill and scholarship, the William Peters House and all of its details were painstakingly reconstructed to their precise original configuration. —JDM

Primitive Hall

First time visitors to the early-eighteenth-century Primitive Hall are often surprised that such a prominent manorial style house was built in such a remote place in the rural countryside of Chester County. Joseph Pennock, its builder, established a homestead house that retains status as one of the county's greatest architectural treasures of any type or era.

The Pennock family first became associated with the land where Primitive Hall stands as early as the 1680s. Mary Collett, one of the first landowners, was married to Christopher Pennock, who in 1684, moved to Pennsylvania from Ireland. The land was passed down to Joseph Pennock, the surviving son of Christopher. Joseph, born in 1677 at Killhouse, Ireland, eventually settled in Pennsylvania in the very early eighteenth century. Considerably later, Pennock, at a rather advanced age, in 1738 constructed his manor house. Joseph acted in several capacities as public servant, including the colonial legislature. He opened his doors to many visitors at Primitive Hall, including Native Americans. When Joseph Pennock died in 1771 at the age of 94, many neighbors and friends mourned his death.

The main section of Primitive Hall, an impressive two-story original brick edifice, has unusually large proportions for a rural home built in the 1730s. The recently constructed rear wing functions for current day support functions. Archeological evidence suggests that a rear wing likely existed at one time. Pennock, determined not to skimp on embellishments, utilized costly Flemish bond brick work on all exterior walls. Short projecting pent roofs above the first story windows appear at the front wall, both end walls, and about one-half of the rear wall. Other refinements are pent eaves at the top of the second story on both end walls. The house, of four-bay construction, has four windows on the front wall's second floor and three windows and a door on the first floor. Most double

Refined architectural expressions were included throughout Primitive Hall. The grand statement made by Joseph Pennock shows through every detail both large and small from the stylish Flemish bond brickwork to the prominent pent eaves and pent roofs.

Above: As in most rooms of the house, the first floor room to the side of the center hall has a corner fireplace. A protective chair rail encircles the entire room.

Right: Looking across a front room to the hall and to the opposite room at the front of the house, numerous mid-eighteenth-century architectural elements are all registered in the mind of the visitor to Primitive Hall. None are subordinate to any other.

hung windows appear oversized, with 15 panes over 15 panes of glass. The exposed foundation wall is stone. Cryptically, cellar sections appear only at each side of the centered hall; they do not connect under the hall. Details large and small attest to the painstaking efforts Joseph Pennock exercised in creating such a grand house.

On the interior, two rooms flank each side of the first floor center hall, which has a brick floor. Interior partitions have no wooden lathe, as plaster is laid directly on the brick of the walls. One of the most prominent features of the interior is the wide open staircase that ascends from the first floor to the attic. The floor plan of the second floor duplicates that of the first floor—two rooms on each side of the hall. Each room has a corner fireplace, some of which have distinctive wooden panels and mantels. —GDH

Acknowledgments

A project of this size and scope requires the help and assistance of many people. We attempt to list them here, but time and space prevent us from listing all.

Thank you to Kelly Smyth, who provided the idea and set up for the frontispiece.

The staff at Rizzoli has worked hard and long at maintaining the overall integrity of this book in a manner that would not be compromised. Thank you to David Morton, Douglas Curran, Charles Miers, Pam Sommers, Jacquie Byrnes, and all the other staff members there. Abigail Sturges and Webb Eaken at Abigail Sturges Graphic Design have turned a heaping pile of images into a well-organized and cohesive volume.

To the homeowners and site personnel who freely gave of their personal time to accommodate us, we say thank you: Washington Crossing Historic Park—Hilary Krueger, Michael Bertheaud, Michelle Matz, Jennifer Glass; Graeme Park-Sir William Keith House—Patricia Mousley, Herb Levy, Sarah Brown; The Highlands Historical Society—Meg Bleecker Blades, Margie Robins, Jennifer April; Pennsbury Manor—Doug Miller, Kimberly McCarty; The Pusey House—Joanne and Harold R. Peden; Peter Wentz House—Dianne Cram, Morgan McMillan, Kimberly Praria; Muhlenberg House—Dr. Shetler; Old Trappe Church—Herbert H. Michel, DD, Pastor; Saint David's Church—Linda Butz; Thomas Massey House—A. Richard Paul; Newlin Grist Mill—H. Dabbs Woodfin; John Chad House and Barnes Brinton House—Ginger Tucker, Judy Linzey; William Brinton House—Barbara B. Clough, Ted Brinton; Gilpin House—Elizabeth Rump; Primitive Hall—Eugene D'orio; Historic Fallsington—Erica Armor.

To those whose homes were unfortunately not included in the final edit for this book go our sincerest apologies; this omission was the unfortunate result of limited space and resources, and should not be construed negatively. To Logan Blackburn, assistant to the photographer, whose duties extended well beyond schlepping lights, a heart warm thank you. To Cynthia Richter who gave her time and knowledge to work with the photographer in developing a working method that would reveal these houses in the best manner, we say thank you.

A very special heart-felt thank you to: Howard Szmolko, Christopher Rebollo, Joan and Isaac Garb, Christopher and Celia Lang, Mitch and Susan Bunkin, Lynn Anderson, Norman Glass, Patty and Rob Sykes, Virginia DeNenno, Eric Pfeifer, Harry Jackalous, Larry Walker, Ruth Ellen Davis, Kathy Wandersee, Penelope Batchelor, Sutter Caine, Nancy Ziegler, Mr. Turner, Betty and Frank Davis, Eleanor and Shaun Miller, Kurt Miller, Joyce and Brooks Kaufman, Adrienne and John Jordan, Laura E. and Clarence L. Prickett, Todd Prickett, Elaine and Malcolm Crooks, Katherine and Bill Marek, David Smith, Kathy Auerbach, Geoffrey Marshall, Thomas Richie, Peggy Weymouth, Claire and Alison Skidmore, Mary DeNadai, Henry Cone, Margaret Schiffer, Christine Witherspoon and Warren Reynolds, David Guilmet, Warren Williams, Kenneth Barlow, Bill Marek Jr, Judy and John Herdig, Candace and Stephen Phillips, Patricia and Randl Bye, Josie, Billy, Monkey … and Buster.

Thanks to Edwin Hild and Patrick Bell of Olde Hope Antiques, Solebury Township. Special thank you to Ruth Van Tassel of Van Tassel / Baumann American Antiques, Historic Sugartown, Chester County. A special thank you to Shelley Schorsch and Clarissa deMuzio of Glen Court Design, a firm located in Jenkintown, PA, for their prompt assistance, excellent resources, and historical expertise on the Florin project.

A very special thank you to Mead Shaffer, who invited the photorapher into his home and provided introductions to people and sites well off the beaten path; he was, and still remains, a constant source of energy, inspiration, and encouragement.

Thank you to Robert Ensminger for sharing his knowledge and expertise on Pennsylvania structures.

A very special thank-you to the staff and directors of the Pennsylvania Historical and Museum Commission at 300 North St. Harrisburg, PA 17120. Without their assistance, guidance, and help this book would not have been possible.

While many of the sites featured in this book are private, some sites are open to the public. These include:

Thompson-Neely House at Washington Crossing Historic Park, administered by the PHMC: 215-493-4076.

The Inn at Phillips Mill: 215-862-2984.

The Eight-Square Schoolhouse: 215-598-3313.

Graeme Park-Sir William Keith House, administered by the PHMC: 215-343-0965.

The Thomas Massey House: 610-353-3644.

The Highlands Mansion and Garden, The Highlands Historical Society: 215-641-2687.

Pennsbury Manor, administered by the PHMC: 215-946-0400.

Historic Fallsington (see introduction): 215-295-6567.

Caleb Pusey House, The Friends of the Caleb Pusey House, Inc: 610-874-5665.

Peter Wentz Farmstead, Montgomery County Department of History and Cultural Arts: 610-584-5104.

Muhlenberg House, Historical Society of Trappe: 610-489-7560.

Newlin Grist Mill, Nicholas Newlin Foundation: 610-459-2359.

John Chad House, Chadds Ford Historical Society: 610-388-7376.

The William Brinton House and Historic Site: 610-399-0913.

Gilpin House at Brandywine Battlefield, Chadds Ford, administered by the PHMC: 610-459-3342.

Barnes-Brinton House, Chadds Ford Historical Society: 610-388-7376.

Primitive Hall Foundation: 610-384-2666.

Moland House: 215-342-6852.

Index